Malta: An Archaeological Guide

Malta:
An Archaeological Guide

D. H. TRUMP

FABER AND FABER LIMITED
LONDON

First published in 1972
by Faber and Faber Limited
3 Queen Square, W.C.1.
Printed in Great Britain
by Ebenezer Baylis and Son, Limited
The Trinity Press, Worcester, and London
All rights reserved

ISBN 0 571 09802 9

Contents

7

Illustrations

PLATES

FOREWORD

The Maltese islands cover only 314 square kilometres, but there is probably no other area of this size in the world with such a number and variety of antiquities. The local stone may have something to do with this, since it is easily worked and so plentiful that there is less call for an abandoned ruin to be demolished for its material than is usual in most places. The climate is mild, and natural weathering correspondingly reduced. Isolation has for long periods, particularly throughout the whole of prehistory, allowed local developments to flourish uninterrupted. It is only in very recent times, when tourism has come to play an important part in the islands' economy, that the archaeology itself has come to be considered, rightly, one of Malta's major assets.

There are many guidebooks to the islands available, none of which can afford to ignore the archaeology, but none of which, amongst the practical information and description of the current scene, can spare the space to give the ancient sites the detailed treatment they deserve, with the background necessary for understanding them.

Research into Malta's past has been going on for three centuries or so, since G. F. Abela's *Della Descritione di Malta* in 1647, albeit in a rather desultory fashion in the early days. Some useful descriptions, such as that of Jacques Houel, and even a little excavation, date to the 1770s. Sir Richard Colt Hoare visited the islands in 1790, and left a brief account. In 1827 and the 1830s, the major clearance of the Ġgantija, Ħaġar Qim and Mnajdra was undertaken, though little material was recovered or information recorded by the excavators. Continuous activity began only in the 1880s, with workers like A. A. Caruana, Albert Mayr and Father Magri. Dr Themistocles Zammit, later knighted, began one of his three brilliant careers (he had others in medicine and education) at the Valletta Museum and at the Hypogeum in 1905. There followed a burst of activity, led by Zammit himself, Dr T. Ashby and E. T. Peet, Dr N. Tagliaferro and others, down to 1914.

The war years saw Zammit's major contribution, the meticulous excavation of the key site of Tarxien. Between the wars, many more of the outlying temple sites were investigated, notably Mġarr in 1923–7. The Museum, too, grew in size and interest. Zammit's death in 1935 was a sad loss, and research languished until the 1950s.

Then, Professor J. D. Evans gave an enormous boost to Maltese archaeology by producing order from the chaos of the prehistoric pottery. At last a relative chronology was available, against which developments, particularly of the temple architecture, could be measured. The present writer, during five years' service with the National Museum, filled out the earlier periods from the evidence excavated at Skorba and was able, with the help of the new technique of radiocarbon dating, to add a more reliable timescale to the pre-historic periods. From 1963, the Italian Missione Archeologica, at Tas-Silġ and San Pawl Milqghi, has been studying the Punic and Roman periods, their researches still continuing.

Throughout, there have been contributions to knowledge from interested amateurs, and it would be ungracious not to mention their collective help, if invidious to single out individuals among so many. Field survey and underwater exploration have benefited particularly in this way.

But it remains true to say, with relief rather than with regret, that the islands' past still bristles with unsolved problems. No attempt is made in the following pages to gloss over what we still do not know, since this adds to, rather than detracts from, the fascination of the subject.

Of the many who have helped in the preparation of this book, three cannot be passed without special mention. Capt. C. G. Zammit, who retired as Director of the Museum Department in 1971, gave unfailing cooperation and encouragement over the years. Professor J. D. Evans helped by discussion and by granting permission to use his new surveys of the monuments. And my wife has made my task the easier in countless ways.

INTRODUCTION

GEOGRAPHY

Malta's geographical position in the Mediterranean can be considered, paradoxically, to have changed drastically in about the 9th century B.C., when the Phoenicians introduced more advanced techniques of navigation. Since then, Malta has found itself at a strategic crossroad, with the main route from the east Mediterranean to the west intersecting a lesser but still important one from Europe to North Africa. Malta's exceptionally fine harbours, of course, add to its importance as both trade centre and naval base. The introduction of air travel has further emphasized its position. As long as seafaring was restricted to coastwise routes, Malta and Gozo were accessible only from Sicily, 80 kilometres to the north. There may have been direct contact with Pantelleria, 210 kilometres to the west, as suggested by the obsidian (p. 43), but this trade probably, and certainly all others, passed along the Sicilian coasts. To interpret this period in relation to the modern situation can only be misleading.

To take the story back to an earlier stage, before man became able to tackle the challenge of the sea at all, Malta was impossibly remote. Our earliest evidence for human occupation goes back to about 4000 B.C. according to conventional radiocarbon dates (but see p. 20). We cannot prove that no one reached the islands before that, but it seems very unlikely from what we know of man's capabilities, or lack of them, elsewhere at this time. Seagoing boats were simply not yet available to him.

One hears frequent mention of Malta's 'land-bridges'. Such there certainly were, at least north to Sicily—they are needed to explain the fossil fauna of Għar Dalam for example—but not, as far as we know, at a period when there were men to take advantage of them. They are of great interest to the geologist and palaeontologist, but of none to the archaeologist.

Malta at present has an area of 243 square kilometres, Gozo 69, Comino 2, and so down to the lesser islets and rocks. Despite the evidence of a rising sea level along the north-east coast, it is probable

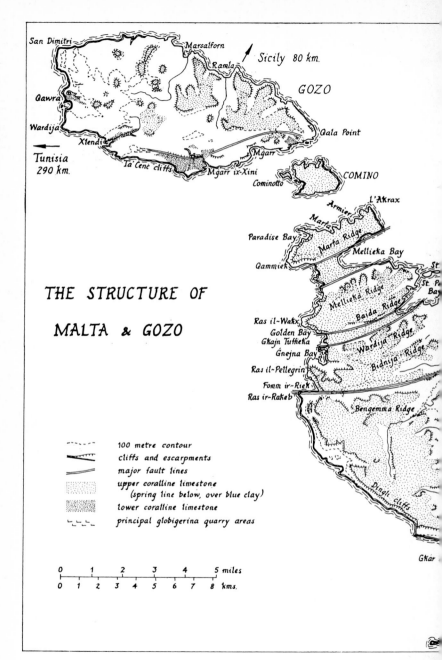

THE STRUCTURE OF

MALTA & GOZO

Legend:

- ------- 100 metre contour
- cliffs and escarpments
- major fault lines
- upper coralline limestone
  (spring line below, over blue clay)
- lower coralline limestone
- principal globigerina quarry areas

Scale:
0 1 2 3 4 5 miles
0 1 2 3 4 5 6 7 8 kms.

Fig. I. Malta and Gozo,

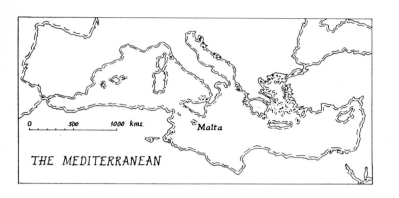

0   500   1000 kms.   Malta

THE MEDITERRANEAN

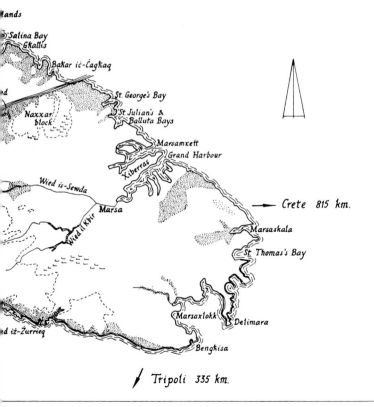

Islands

Salina Bay
Għallis

Baħar iċ-Ċagħaq

St. George's Bay

St Julian's &
Balluta Bays

Marsamxett
Grand Harbour

Xiberras

Wied is-Sewda
Naxxar
block

Marsa

Wied il Kbir

Crete 815 km.

Marsaskala

St. Thomas's Bay

d iż-Żurrieq

Marsaxlokk   Delimara

Bengħisa

Tripoli 335 km.

tructure and position

that over the 6,000 years we are concerned with, Malta has changed little
in shape and size. Surface appearance is another matter. That serious soil
erosion has taken place is shown both by rock surfaces now stripped bare
and by inlets of the sea silted up. But again the results can be exag-
gerated, or at least misdated. Those rock surfaces on which cart-ruts
(p. 31) are now visible must have lost, or all but lost, any soil cover they
may once have had before the period when the ruts were cut. The same
applies to tree cover. For the temple period there is still much un-
certainty, though we could argue that timber must have been readily
available then. Deforestation and subsequent soil loss may well have
had much to do with the temples' sudden end. Evidence will be cited
(p. 88) for the islands' vegetation having taken on virtually its present-
day composition before 1000 B.C.

What cannot have altered over the period of human occupation is the
basic structure of the island (Fig. 1). It may be likened to a huge ham
sandwich. The lower slice of bread is represented by the lower coralline
limestone, a semicrystalline deposit laid down in clear but shallow seas,
rich in marine fossils. The golden globigerina limestone, a deep sea ooze
deposit, appears as a generous layer of butter. The ham, a little past its
best perhaps, can be equated with the blue clay, fine debris washed off a
neighbouring land mass and deposited on the sea bed off its shores. A
thin layer of greensand then serves as a smear of mustard before the
sandwich is capped with the upper coralline limestone, as like the lower
as two slices of bread off the same loaf. All belong to the Miocene period.

Since then, however, the sandwich has received a good deal of rough
handling. For a start, it is markedly tilted, higher on the west, lower on
the east. The bays and inlets of the north and east coast are the drowned
valleys resulting. Though it has not crumpled much, it has torn
through on a number of fault lines, to displace the strata relative to each
other. The most prominent fault is that followed by the Victoria Lines
and clearly visible at the head of Fomm ir-Rieh. Another pushed the
Ta' Ċenċ plateau up to overlook the centre of Gozo, and a third carried
a strip of the south coast of Malta down, leaving the cleft of the Wied
ix-Xaqqa on the Għar Lapsi road. Other faults again explain the alterna-
tion of parallel ridges and valleys across north Malta.

A further phenomenon to mention is karstic erosion. Chemical dissolution, in which the rock is dissolved by water and carried away, is
more important in limestone country than the grinding action of
flowing water. There are many caves in the island, though few of them
reach any great size. Several circular depressions represent enormous

collapsed caves or enlarged swallowholes. The Maqluba at Qrendi and the Inland Sea, Qawra, west Gozo, are two striking examples of this.

The geology has two effects. The structure of the islands dictate their shape in detail as well as in general. On Malta's west coast, the whole sequence is exposed in a series of cliffs. The plateau area, and the flat-topped Gozitan hills, are surviving fragments of the upper coralline limestone. The clay beneath forms easily eroded slopes around the high ground, and traps percolating rainwater to provide the islands' vital springs. The gentler slopes of the lower, eastern, end of Malta and the centre of Gozo are the results of the softer globigerina of which they are composed.

Secondly, the nature of the rock dictates the uses to which it can be put. The coralline is intractable, can be used in the slabs in which it is found but can be cut to shape only with great difficulty. It supports thin soils which are easily swept away to leave bare rock. The clay is useful for making pottery and mudbricks, and when not too steeply sloping grows good crops. But its main economic value is certainly for the springs of water which break out above it. The globigerina is an excellent, easily worked building stone, and in addition can be broken down with patience into good arable soil. Alluvial plains are few and small, the Marsa and Burmarrad being the only ones of any size.

The islands enjoy, as one might expect, a Mediterranean climate, with mild winters and hot, dry summers. Rainfall is moderate (average 58 cm.) but very variable from year to year. Humidity tends to be high, and St Paul has not been the only visitor to comment on the strength of the wind.

The present population is a little over 300,000. Comparison with some of the Aegean islands today, for example, would suggest that Malta and Gozo might have supported a population of the order of 10,000 in antiquity, a very different figure. This cannot by the nature of things be anything more than a rough and ready estimate, but some sort of figure is needed for any assessment of the implications of the temples or the Hypogeum.

OUTLINE HISTORY

As mentioned in the geographical introduction, there is nothing to suggest that man reached the islands until something like 6,000 years ago. Though there is always at least a faint possibility that material of the Old Stone Age may yet come to light, we begin the story with the New Stone Age or Neolithic.

The earliest inhabitants we know of were farmers, and to have reached Malta they must have been sailors too. They brought with them crops like barley, two primitive forms of wheat, emmer and club wheat, and lentils. Remains of all these have been found at Skorba. Their boats were large and seaworthy enough for the transport of domestic animals, large cattle, sheep, goats and pigs, doubtless securely trussed to prevent accidents. They made and used pottery of the Ghar Dalam style, with impressed decoration identical with that of the Stentinello Ware found commonly in Sicily. This is itself a local version of the Impressed Wares which occur widely round the coasts of the Central and West Mediterranean in the settlements of the first farmers. The discovery of these skills—pottery making, husbandry and navigation— must have taken place back in the East Mediterranean, where the wild ancestors of the cereals, sheep and goats were to be found, but the routes by which they spread are still imperfectly known.

The date for the arrival of these first settlers in Malta is set by radio-carbon at or slightly before 4000 B.C., using the conventional calculation. Radiocarbon as a dating method, however, has recently been drastically reassessed as a result of careful comparisons with other methods, in particular dendrochronology, or tree-ring counting. We now know that 4000 B.C. must be a serious underestimate, and that a more accurate figure would be 5000 or a little after. It is worth noting wryly that the archaeologists' unaided guess was about 2300 B.C., a figure still occa-sionally misleadingly quoted. Until the exact corrections have been determined, there is international agreement, which will be followed here, to continue quoting radiocarbon dates as before, so that at least they can be fairly compared with one another.

These early immigrants maintained some contact with Sicily and beyond, for certain raw materials found in the archaeological deposits like obsidian and ochre do not occur naturally in Malta. But on the whole the settlers went their own way, and their pottery is soon recognizably different from any being produced elsewhere. At Skorba, two phases, which are so far represented only by odd sherds from other sites, were distinguished. Grey Skorba has virtually no decoration and Red Skorba little, apart from the unmistakable bright red slip which covers its pottery's surface.

At about 3200 B.C. there is a marked change which signals the end of the first period of Maltese prehistory. Perhaps it is to be explained by the arrival of new people from outside. Two new styles of pottery appear, to characterize the Żebbuġ phase, a grey ware with broad scratched decoration, and a cream ware with red painting. The designs in the two are closely similar, including highly schematized little men. The scratched ware in particular shows similarities to the San Cono-Piano Notaro Ware of the Early Copper Age in Sicily. Once again, however, Malta soon began to go its own peculiar way.

A short transitional phase, Mġarr, leads to the particularly interesting one named after the Ġgantija. The pottery designs are now worked in a light scratched line, and are based on a pleasing use of converging and diverging curves, conveniently labelled 'comets'. Great variety and originality are apparent. Even more important is the development through this period, roughly 2800 to 2400 B.C., of the very distinctive Maltese temples. These are discussed in detail in a later section. Tombs are now certainly of the shaft and chamber type. It is a phase of both experiment and achievement.

Another short transitional phase, Saflieni, leads on to the final one of this middle period, called after the Tarxien temples. In both pottery and architecture, experiment along the old lines stops. The temples follow each other in standard form, and the now very finely scratched ware shows the same volute pattern endlessly repeated. Other techniques of decoration appear, it is true, but none recaptures the spontaneity and imagination of the Ġgantija comets. Only in the modelling and carving of figurines does one find fresh artistic activity, producing figures from 2·75 metres high down to fascinating little heads under a couple of centimetres.

It is a very difficult period to assess objectively, because looking back on it we are perhaps excessively conscious of its impending end. There is a great temptation to look for hints of weakness and instability before the moment of collapse, whether they were really there or not. The increasing evidence for a priesthood, for example, could be quoted as a possible cause of internal revolt. The excessive temple building might imply neglect of the precious soil of the fields. It could have depleted dangerously the local timber resources, again encouraging soil erosion. To the unprovable 'mights' and 'perhapses' we could add drought, plague, religious hysteria even, or foreign invasion.

Despite the progressive lengthening of the Tarxien Cemetery phase of the Early Bronze Age, as a result of new techniques of dating, the changeover, now placed about 2000 B.C., still appears to have been sudden and extraordinarily complete. It remains true that there is no slightest trace of continuity between the builders of the temples and the people who turned their ruins to other uses, or simply ignored them. If the newcomers subjugated their predecessors, one would have expected details of the rich earlier culture to survive, the techniques of pot-making if not the pot forms or designs for example, the settlement sites if not the architecture, some sanctity clinging to the temples if not a continuation of the full ceremonies and rituals. As it is, judging from the cultural evidence of the Tarxien Cemetery phase, Malta may well have been completely deserted when the Bronze Age folk arrived to open the third and last prehistoric period.

The origins of the newcomers are almost as mysterious. Related pottery styles appear at about the same time in Sicily, Lipari, the heel of Italy and in western Greece, but where their makers came from and why they came requires more research than has yet been given to the problem. What marks them off most clearly from the temple builders in Malta is their use of metal, daggers and axes of bronze being found with the cremated ashes of their dead.

About the middle of the second millennium, the Borġ in-Nadur phase opens. This may be the result of another immigration, but could instead be a local development within the islands. Changes in the pottery, to red-slipped bowls and pedestalled vessels with cut-out decoration, are in themselves of no great significance unless a specific source can be found for them elsewhere. More important historically is the increase in evidence for warfare. The sites of this phase are nearly all on incommodious but secure cliff-girt hill tops (Nuffara, Baħrija). Where the natural defences were inadequate, massive built walls were added (Borġ in-Nadur itself, Wardija ta' San Ġorġ, Qala Hill, Fawwara). Malta had become a very different place to live in from what it had been in the temple period. It was during this phase, too, that the cart-ruts were formed.

The last prehistoric phase is another minor one, apparently not affecting the whole island. Baħrija itself is the only important site. Here, new pottery styles with Calabrian connections suggest the arrival and absorption of a band perhaps of refugees from Southern Italy about 900 B.C.

Some time in the 9th century, the Phoenicians, on their trading ventures into the West Mediterranean, came upon the island of Malta. They must very quickly have realized its possibilities. For the mid-sea routes they could now follow, Malta, with its excellent harbours, provided a perfect base. Before long, we begin to find the first of the many Phoenician rock-cut tombs. The nature of their occupation is uncertain in the absence of recognized settlements, and there are many problems. No Phoenician material has yet turned up on a native site. The earliest known tomb was found at Siġġiewi, not, as one would have expected, somewhere close to the harbours. Certainly by the 8th century, as shown by tombs around Rabat, Phoenician control had spread over the whole island, presumably to prevent any threat to the vital harbours.

When the Phoenician homeland went down before the Assyrians and Babylonians, Carthage took over the western colonies and trading posts, and we talk of the Punic period to mark the change. Malta became of even greater strategic importance to the Carthaginians after their enemies, the Greeks, colonized eastern Sicily in the 8th and 7th centuries.

The Carthaginian hold on the island was broken by Titus Sempronius Longus in 218 B.C., during the Second Punic War. But cultural changes lagged well behind political ones, and Malta remained Punic to all intents and purposes for a couple of centuries or more after the Roman conquest. Its renowned temple to Juno, probably Tas-Silġ, is mentioned by Cicero as one of the victims of Verres's spoliations. The incidental information that Maltese textiles had a high reputation is worth noting.

In A.D. 60, Paul came unwillingly to Malta. The account of his arrival and stay in the last two chapters of the Acts of the Apostles is brief and circumstantial, but still difficult to tie in with the known topography and archaeology (pp. 144 and 145). One of the most significant remarks is that the Maltese were 'barbarians', which in the context meant only that they spoke neither Greek nor Latin. Surviving inscriptions show that their language was still, after 270 years of Roman rule, Punic.

Later classical references are few and unenlightening. The Latin writers seem to have been interested in Malta only for its breed of diminutive dogs. The archaeology tells us a little more. There was considerable prosperity, which lasted well into the 4th century at least, as shown by the great number of catacombs. Christianity was present, but to what extent cannot now be determined. The evidence for Judaism is no less strong.

There follows a long and obscure period. Byzantine history and a few coins argue for an occupation of Malta by the Eastern Empire in the 7th century. Islam arrived under the banners of Ibn Khafadsha in

A.D. 870. The cross returned with the Norman Count Roger from Sicily in 1090. There followed a succession of European dynasties, Angevin, Swabian, Aragonese and Castilian, but none has left any lasting material mark on the island. Some Moslem tombstones (pp. 113 and 151) and pottery of North African affinity are all there is to show for that period of history: the language, p. 34, is another matter. And of the early Middle Ages we have only some Sicilian and Italian pottery fragments. Upstanding remains appear only in the 15th, at earliest later 14th, century.

Malta shot from obscurity to fame almost by accident. The Knights of St John of Jerusalem, expelled from Rhodes by the Turks in 1522, sought a base from which to continue their fight for Christendom. Charles V of Spain, uninterested in Malta and embarrassed by the acquisition, again almost by accident, of Tripoli, used the one as a bribe to relieve himself of the other. So in 1530 the Knights, with many misgivings, came to Malta. Their wealth, from their properties all over Europe, poured into the island. The price the Maltese had to pay, in their sufferings during the Turkish attack in 1565, was high, but was not asked again. But the Knights became more and more of an anachronism and surrendered without a blow when faced by the revolutionary fervour of the French in 1798. The Maltese soon found it was a change for the worse and they rose against their new masters. The French could not hold the countryside, but nor could the Maltese recover Valletta until they had entered into alliance with the naval power of Britain.

From 1801 to 1964, Malta formed a part of the British Empire, with a varying amount of say in its own government. The Second Siege, of 1940–3, was added to its annals, with the assault coming this time mainly from the air. In 1964, Malta became an independent state within the Commonwealth.

TEMPLES

The temples are Malta's most important antiquities, and there is much to be said for putting together our information here, whilst leaving their individual descriptions to appear in the appropriate places later.

Function. There can now be very little argument but that they really were temples. Their monumental size and the nature of their contents would seem to exclude domestic use completely. Only one, Tarxien, has produced human burials, and those of a subsequent period. Nor, then, are they tombs, though it will be suggested under Origins below that there may well be an underlying connection. On the positive side, structures which can most easily be interpreted as altars abound. Tarxien has yielded (p. 68) the clearest evidence of animal sacrifice. Though the smaller figurines are clearly not conclusive, the great 'fat lady' at the same site can surely only be a cult statue.

Deity. Almost certainly, this statue at Tarxien represents the deity to whom these temples were raised. The same figure can be recognized in more modest, though still substantial, stone carvings from the same site, Ħaġar Qim, and less commonly elsewhere. There is less certainty about other figures, which could equally be identified as attendants, worshippers, ex votos, etc. It must be admitted at the start that to describe her, as is usually done, as a goddess or 'fat lady' may be no more than male prejudice. The sex is not explicitly indicated. Corpulence in women is frequently, though mistakenly, held to be a sign of fertility, and the same symbolism can be clearly seen elsewhere. Note in particular the bull and sow reliefs from Tarxien (p. 72) and carved stone phalli from that (p. 47) and other sites. If we call her a goddess from now on, this is a matter of probability and convenience rather than proof. That she may have a more sinister aspect is discussed under Origins below. The Ġgantija snake (p. 150) and the common libation holes point unmistakably to the underworld.

Form. Leaving aside sites of ruinous or irregular form, five classes of temple plan can be recognized. The individual sites are listed in the accompanying table. All are set in a roughly D-shaped structure with massive external wall, and usually with the entrance at the centre of a slightly concave façade. A passage leads into a central court. Then:

(1) Lobed. The court expands fairly irregularly into curvilinear chambers.

(2) Trefoil or three-apse. Three swelling D-shaped chambers open symmetrically off the court. The central apse was later walled off, and the side apses may be partially or completely screened too.

(3) Five-apse. A second pair of lateral apses is added in front of the first, giving a second passage on the central axis.

(4) Four-apse. The central apse is reduced to a mere niche, very much smaller than the side apses.

(5) Six-apse. A third pair of lateral apses is added, the central niche remaining small.

Table: **Temple Development**

Class	*Sites*	*Plan*	*Phase*
1. Lobed	Kordin III E.		Ġgantija
	Mġarr E.		Saflieni
2. Trefoil	Kordin III W.		Ġgantija
	Skorba W.		,,
	Buġibba		,,
	Mnajdra E.	Fig. 17	,,
	Santa Verna		,,
	Ġgantija S?	Fig. 32	,,
3. Five-apse	Ġgantija S.	,,	,,
	Tarxien Far E.	Fig. 12	,,
	Ħaġar Qim N.		Tarxien
	Ta' Marżiena		?
4. Four-apse	Ġgantija N.	Fig. 32	Ġgantija
	Tarxien S.	Fig. 12	Early Tarxien
	Tarxien E.	,,	,,
	Mnajdra S.	Fig. 17	,,
	Mnajdra C.	,,	Tarxien
	Skorba E.		,,
	Borġ in-Nadur		,,
	Xrobb il-Għaġin		,,
5. Six-apse	Tarxien C.	Fig. 12	,,

This classification is simply based on the plans, but is supported by correlation with the pottery development to a great extent. Classes 1 to 3 were built in the Ġgantija phase, with only two exceptions (Mġarr East, class 1, Saflieni phase; Ħagar Qim N, class 3, Tarxien). The chronological order of these three classes within the phase remains hypothetical. Class 4 belongs to the Tarxien phase, again with a single but less certain exception. Ġgantija North produced no sherds later than the Ġgantija phase from the small cuts made beneath its floors, so was probably built before the end of that phase, or at latest very early in the next. The same is true of the partial temple plans attached to Ħaġar Qim Central, which have class 4 niches if not the full number of apses. Ġgantija North is certainly stratigraphically later than Ġgantija South. Tarxien Central, the only member of class 5, is also of the Tarxien phase and later than its four-apse neighbours. Ḥaġar Qim Central and Tas-Silġ have been omitted from the table as it is impossible to decide whether their second door replaces a class 3 apse or a class 4 niche.

The emphasis on decoration in the first pair of apses suggests that the screening of the inner apse and the adding of an extra pair may have a common cause, a change in ritual calling for a private, inner chamber separated from the public, outer ones. This point will be taken up again shortly.

The frequently repeated suggestion that the plan of the temples is based on the shape of the goddess herself has no factual basis.

Origins. There is nothing looking remotely like one of these temples outside the Maltese islands, so we cannot use 'foreign influence' to explain them away. The almost complete absence of imported pottery further strengthens the argument. Professor Evans's theory that they could be copies above ground of the rock-cut tombs of Xemxija type (p. 143) below ground has much to recommend it. The similarity in plan is certainly suggestive, if not conclusive. The earliest tombs date from before, but not too far before, the earliest temples. Further support comes from the Hypogeum, a copy of a built temple carved out of the rock. But the Hypogeum is cemetery as well as temple, emphasizing a link between the two.

There are broad hints, then, that the goddess had an interest in death as well as fertility. The two are not so contradictory as appears at first sight if death was looked upon as a prelude to rebirth. A close link between tomb and temple seems certain, but the strongest argument, perhaps, remains that if we cannot explain the temples in this way, we cannot explain them at all.

Distribution. Twenty-three classifiable temples are known, of which six stand alone, ten are in pairs, and there is one group of three and one of four. Five more structures of similar type have irregular plans, and there are at least twenty scatters of megalithic blocks with sherds of the appropriate period which could represent the last vestiges of former temples. Tas-Silġ came to light as recently as 1964, but it is on the whole unlikely that many more remain to be discovered. The number completely destroyed we shall never know.

No particular pattern emerges from their distribution. There is a marked cluster at the head of Grand Harbour, and again around Xagħra in Gozo. Equally obvious are blank areas across the centre of

Malta and in west Gozo, but we cannot be sure that these are not accidents of survival or discovery.

Date. In the sequence described above, the temples span from early in the Ġgantija phase to the end of that of Tarxien. Using conventional radiocarbon dates, this covers a period of some eight centuries, 2800–2000 B.C., or, as provisionally corrected (see p. 20), something like 3500–2500 B.C. For comparative purposes, we should now place the Great Pyramid of Egypt about 2575 B.C., the Palaces of Crete about 2000 and Stonehenge about 2300.

Construction. The finer temples still stand to some height, and as well as the ruins themselves we have a few remarkable contemporary models and engravings to show us what they once looked like (Fig. 2). The

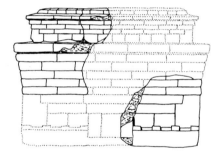

Fig. 2. Contemporary model of a temple façade from Tarxien. Original height 33 cm

principles of construction are simple enough for anyone prepared to manipulate slabs of rock up to twenty tons in weight, the megalithic technique. The results can still be remarkably sophisticated. The walls are formed of blocks of stone propped on end or on edge as orthostats. Outer walls are usually of unhewn coralline uprights with alternately face or edge projecting. In the façade, all orthostats have the face exposed, and the end blocks are higher and notched at the inner corner to take the first of the horizontal courses which cap them.

Internal walls are either of piled rough coralline blocks, or well-cut globigerina slabs set as orthostats. The former would have been rendered in red painted plaster. Upper courses internally and externally are set in the more usual horizontal fashion. All walls consist of two faces, each only one stone thick, the space between being packed with earth or rubble. Where space allowed, the packing would be omitted to leave subsidiary chambers within the wall thickness.

Doorways and passages all use the trilithon principle, two orthostats parallel to each other to support a horizontal lintel. Frequently doorways consist of a 'porthole', in which access is through a rectangular hole in the centre of a slab. Doors are framed within nesting trilithons, each set of three slabs being enclosed within a larger set which projects slightly beyond it. Finishing and decoration of structural elements were carried out after erection. Tarxien gave some evidence on the methods of handling the large blocks (p. 74).

It is noticeable how rarely a straight line is used. Instead, all the blocks appear to swell slightly, like the sag of a soft cheese, giving an impression of comfortable solidity.

Some of the relief decoration is such delicate work that it is difficult to believe that it could have been carried out using only stone tools. However, with the exception of a little gold inlay in a bead from Tarxien, no metal has ever been found in the relevant level of any temple site. This is surprising at this date, and is of course only negative evidence. Perhaps metal was excluded from the temples for religious reasons. Settlement sites might give a fairer picture, but so far they have escaped discovery.

Roofing. Though no roof survives today, roofs can be assumed from the absence of weathering on decorated blocks when first exposed, from the use of painted plaster, from the oversailing of walls, and from representations in the Hypogeum and the Mġarr model (p. 43). The rough walling of, for example, the Ġgantija could never have supported the weight of a corbelled or beehive vault in stone. At a certain level it was probably completed with a flat roof of beams, brushwood and clay. This may be implied at the Hypogeum, and is supported by the heavy burning at Tarxien and the distribution of clay, ash and charcoal on the floors of Skorba.

The problem is different with ashlar masonry. Here the walls can definitely be seen to curve out in places at Haġar Qim, Mnajdra and Tarxien. At Mnajdra, the whole blocks, not just their exposed faces, slope in towards the chamber. The third chamber left of Tarxien Central (p. 73) is even more explicit. The first block from the left of the course of stones above the orthostats is original. The marked inward slope of its upper surface shows that it cannot technically be part of a corbelled vault. The elements of this must slope outwards, to carry the thrust out into the supporting packing. An inward slope implies an arch, though not necessarily in the vertical plane as we are now accustomed to. Here it is in the horizontal plane, each course being self-supporting, locked by the inward thrust. A pair of apses thus forms the two halves of a circular horizontal arch, separated into an oval by the straight lintel blocks of the trilithon passages, doorways and niches. Above the lintels, convergence of the vault is no longer possible, since straight sections of walling are not locked but held only by friction. At this level, the reduced aperture would have been completed with rafters and some kind of thatch. Imaginative reconstructions in stone throughout are architecturally impossible, at least over the larger chambers, because of the enormous weight of stone necessary. The horizontal arch, it must be repeated however, is practicable only with well-dressed masonry.

Ritual. All the temples are divided into a closed or private inner part and a 'public' outer one; Tarxien, Mnajdra and Ħaġar Qim have 'oracle' holes; both imply some special or privileged group, in short a priesthood. Tarxien, as has been said, gave fairly explicit evidence for animal sacrifice. This might be the best place to emphasize that there is nothing to suggest human sacrifice. Tarxien and the Ġgantija had hearths or bowls reddened by fire, perhaps for burning aromatic herbs. Altars and libation holes are common in all temples. The forecourts

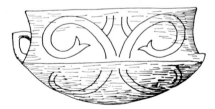

Fig. 3. Offering bowl, Tarxien phase, *c.* 2200 B.C. Diameter 20 cm

imply some activities out in front of the temples. Vast numbers of handled cups, best interpreted as offering bowls (Fig. 3), have been recovered from the less disturbed sites, but always broken. The Hypogeum, as will be seen, offers several more intriguing possibilities. The orientation of the temples could be significant, did one but know of what. On these slender and unreliable foundations, one can reconstruct in imagination whatever ceremonies one wishes.

Siting. The entrances of the temples almost invariably face somewhere between due east and due south. Tarxien Central is the most important exception, facing a little west of south, and Ta'-Silġ is a special case discussed on p. 79. This orientation seems little affected by the natural slope, though most temples are either on level ground or face down a slope. They rarely occupy the highest available, or even the most commanding, position.

Builders. Our understanding of the temples is greatly hampered by the fact that we have not found the settlements of their builders. The huts identified at Skorba were abandoned at the time the temple there was built, and were comparatively slight structures. Others, then, could easily escape notice, particularly if their sites are still occupied by the present villages as would be quite likely.

In the tombs, we can look at the mortal remains of these people. Unlike their successors in Malta from the Bronze Age on, they are a long-headed race, a branch of the Mediterranean stock widespread in this region today. They have disappeared, however, from Malta itself, where they were replaced during the Bronze Age by a round-headed people of Alpine affinity.

Destruction. At the end of the Tarxien phase, the temples went out of use. At Tarxien and to a lesser extent at Skorba there were signs of fire. At Skorba and Borġ in-Nadur, squatters of later periods moved into the ruins. At Tarxien, after a period of abandonment, part of the temple was given over to a cemetery. Only at Tas-Silġ has continuity of sanctity been claimed, and there, subsequent remodelling of the site has been so drastic as to make proof impossible. The collapse of the temple culture appears to have been rapid and complete. Here is another unsolved problem, which has already been touched upon in another context.

CART-RUTS

One of the most intriguing aspects of Maltese archaeology is that of the so-called cart-ruts. These are parallel grooves in bare rock representing traffic long before the present landscape pattern was established. They run in pairs, sometimes for long distances, often forking or combining like railway sidings, until they disappear beneath fields, roads or houses, over cliff edges or into the sea. The better groups will be discussed in their place (pp. 118, 126, 130) but it is worth putting together here what is known about them, and what remains still a mystery.

Location. Outside Malta, they have been reported from Cyrenaica, Sicily and Sardinia, but even less research has been done on them in those places, so we cannot expect an answer to Maltese problems to be supplied from outside. In Malta and Gozo they occur on practically every exposure of upper or lower coralline or globigerina limestone. If they are commoner in highland Malta, this is probably only because of the larger areas of bare rock there. For the same reason, Gozo has few—on Ta' Ċenċ, south-east of Xewkija, and east of Qala.

Tracing the ruts across country for plotting on to large-scale maps is a very satisfying sport, more humane than most, particularly on bright winter days with their invigorating blend of warm sun and cool air. Much of the new information in the following paragraphs comes from such excursions, in my case disguised, if only very thinly, as work.

Behaviour. A common pattern—one cannot say rule—is for them to climb from one cultivated valley, cross a ridge by the most convenient route, and descend to vanish below the fields of the next valley. This is why they are so frequently found beside modern roads, which are, of course, doing exactly the same thing, short of vanishing. The prominent group running from Salina, past Tal-Qadi and up to San Pawl tat-Tarġa might have carried salt, or any other sea product. Most can be explained by regular agricultural activities.

Where they run over cliffs (Għar Żerrieq, Ras il-Pellegrin) or into the sea (St George's and Mellieħa Bays), they reappear within a few score yards, and cannot be quoted as evidence for land-bridges. In some places, as near San Lawrenz on Ġebel Ciantar, ruts start off clearly across bare rock, but become progressively fainter until they disappear. In the absence of evidence for erosion of the rock, this must indicate the former existence of soil cover, since swept away.

Date. Erosion and submersion imply some lapse of time, but it need not be very great. Better evidence comes from examples of ruts being cleanly cut by, and therefore older than, Punic tombs (at Għar il-Kbir, Mtarfa, Benġemma, etc.). Better still, at a few sites (Borġ in-Nadur, Qala Hill, Fawwara) ruts clearly run up to the entrances of Bronze Age villages, whereas there is no known association with any earlier or later site. We can, then, place them securely in the later Bronze Age.

Function. The pairing of ruts, and their behaviour relative to the topography, make them certainly a means of vehicular communication. The clumsy term requires an apology, and will be explained in the next paragraph. At San Pawl tat-Tarġa, one rut has been tapped to carry rain run-off into a cistern, but this must be secondary. Exceptionally, also, a few show signs of deepening by water action. Most ruts make absolutely no sense for water catchment.

Vehicle. Probably we must envisage a 'slide-car' or travois, in which two poles are supported at one end, drag along the ground at the other, and support a load in the middle. Evidence is hard to adduce, but all alternatives yet suggested can be rejected for one reason or another. A sledge with fixed runners could not turn some of the sharp bends encountered, notably the hairpins at San Pawl tat-Tarġa. Wheels could not negotiate those ruts the gauge of which, i.e. the distance separating the two ruts of a single pair, has been found to vary by some centimetres around an average 1·30 metres. They would inevitably have locked or been wrenched off. Further, a wheel grinds far more from the side of its rut than it removes by crushing from the bottom, producing a much broader and shallower groove.

Wear. The profile of the ruts is, indeed, their most distinctive feature. The deepest recorded is cut 60 cms. into the rock, yet is still only some 40 cms. wide at the top. 5 to 8 cms. is usual for the bottom. These are the result of wear, not of deliberate cutting, although shallow grooves appear to have been pecked on Xemxija Hill (p. 143) to start a pair of ruts. These, however, never came into use or the pecking would have been smoothed away.

This wear tells us two further things about the vehicle. Since the sides of the ruts are symmetrical, the sliding poles must have been parallel, supported by a cross-bar rather than lashed together and splayed. And the depth of wear becomes credible only if we suppose that the poles were somehow shod with stone, probably simply by wedging a rock into a hole cut in the wood for the purpose. Where both are smooth, stone slides on stone far more easily than wood on stone. The point of keeping carefully to the same ruts, however deep they become, is now obvious. The wear too is shared fairly between rut and

3

stone 'shoe', instead of falling almost entirely on the pole, wood for which was probably in short supply.

Sidings. Where ruts fork, it will be noticed that one pair is usually appreciably deeper than the other, showing that they were successive rather than contemporary. For some reason, a route was changed slightly, and gradually the new ruts wore deeper to leave the old ones stranded at a higher level. But multiplication to the extent it can be seen at 'Clapham Junction' requires more explanation than that, and more than we are yet in a position to give.

Traction. This remains the outstanding problem. Even where ruts are worn to a depth of 60 cms., there is never the slightest trace of wear from whatever it was that pulled these vehicles. With modern ruts, wear from the hooves of the draught animal can be seen as early as wear from the wheels. Even bare human feet would soon produce at the very least a polish on the rock surface. Simple experiment soon shows that walking on the bottom of the rut is out of the question. The absence of wear applies outside the ruts as well as between them. To compound the mystery, there are cases, the best at Qallilija (p. 126), where ruts climb for short distances slopes as steep as 45°. To use a hackneyed phrase, the mind boggles.

So the ruts can be taken securely to represent communication routes, probably mainly agricultural, almost certainly of the later 2nd millennium B.C., perhaps worn by slide-cars, on highly likely stone runners, drawn by something making no contact with the ground—flying geese perhaps?

LANGUAGE

The Maltese language is a fascinating one, but its difficulties need not worry visitors. English is very widely spoken. In place names, the pronunciation follows the spelling closely. The only points to watch are the following:

aj — as English 'i' in 'tie'.

c — hard, usually replaced by k; ċ — soft, as English 'ch'.

g — hard; ġ — soft, as English 'j'.

għ = Arabic 'għajn', virtually unpronounced (except in 'Għargħur', where both appear as hard g's).

h — unpronounced; ħ (H) — aspirated, as normal English 'h'.
j — hard, as English consonantal 'y'.
q = Arabic 'qoph', a glottal stop, as Cockney 'tt' in 'butter'. English 'k' gives a recognized but not very close approximation.
x — English 'sh'.
z — hard, as in English 'ts'; ż — soft, as English 'z'.

This should help visitors past such problems as 'Ħagar Qim', 'Ġgantija', 'Taċ-Ċagħqi', 'San Pawl Milqgħi' and even 'Għaxaq'. 'Tal Qroqqa' may require a little more practice.

The language can be described loosely as a blend of North African Arabic (grammar and roughly half the vocabulary) and Sicilian Italian (the other half of the vocabulary), with a sprinkle of words from other sources, particularly of recent years English. Do not be surprised when a flood of Maltese is interrupted by 'carburettor' or 'income tax'. The old view that traces of Phoenician survive in it is not supported by recent research.

The Arabic element is the one which makes it seem so strange. The word roots consist of three or four consonants, among which the vowels appear to an Indo-European speaker to frolic quite wantonly. Few would recognize in the place names L'Imrieħel and Tal Merħla the same noun (meaning 'flock') or in 'iswed' and 'sewda' the same adjective (meaning 'black').

A few words occuring commonly in place names are given with their English equivalents:

abjad, bajada	white
aħmar, ħamra	red
baħar	sea, bay
blata	rock
ġebel	rocky hill
għajn	spring
għar	cave
ħal (short for raħal)	village
irdum	slope below cliffs
kbir	large
tal, ta'	of the
wied	valley
xagħra	rocky plateau
zgħir	small

Another difficulty for visitors is that several towns and villages have alternative names. A short list of these might be helpful too:

Valletta	Il Belt (the City)
Mdina	Notabile
Victoria	Rabat (Gozo)
Vittoriosa	Il Birgu (= Italian Borgo)
Cospicua	Bormla
Senglea	L'Isla (= Italian Isola, island)
Pawla	Raħal il Ġdid (the new village)
Marsaskala	Wied il Għajn

ADMISSION TO SITES

The major archaeological sites in Malta and Gozo are under the care of the Museum Department. There are various categories.

I   The National Museum, Valletta. Hours: 1st October to 15th June—8.30 a.m. to 1 p.m., 2 p.m. to 4.30 p.m.; 16th June to 30th September—8.30 a.m. to 1 p.m., 2 p.m. to 5 p.m. Closed on Sunday afternoons and public holidays. Admission: adults 2/–, young people to age eighteen 1/–.

II   Għar Dalam Cave and Museum
      Tarxien Temples
      Ħal Saflieni Hypogeum
      The Roman Villa Museum
      St Paul's Catacombs
Hours: as National Museum. Admission: adults 1/–, under eighteen 6d.

III   The Gozo Museum
       Ġgantija Temples
Hours: 1st October to 15th June—8.30 a.m. to noon, 1 p.m. to 4.30 p.m.; 16th June to 30th September—8.30 a.m. to noon. Closed on public holidays. Admission as category II.

IV   Ħaġar Qim. Always open. Custodian on duty during same hours as National Museum. No admission charge.

V   Ta' Ħaġrat Temples, Mġarr. Key at Mġarr Police Station, available at any time. No charge.
      Roman Baths, Għajn Tuffieħa. Often open, but key at next farm

if not, available at any time. No charge but a small tip is in order here.

Tas-Silġ. Permission required from the National Museum, key with Mr Carabott at the farm adjacent to the San Nikola Chapel, 500 metres along the Żejtun road.

Buġibba Temple. Apply to the Dolmen Hotel.

Skorba Temples, San Pawl Milqgħi, the catacombs at Salina, Tal Mintna (Mqabba), Ħal Resqun (Luqa) and Abbatija tad-Dejr (Rabat). Keys at the National Museum.

VI All other sites, of which Mnajdra is the most important, are open at all times.

VII Privately owned sites of importance are few, but include St Agatha's Catacombs (open 8 a.m. to 6 p.m., entrance 1/–).

GENERAL INFORMATION

Malta is easily accessible by air from Britain, with non-stop BEA flights daily from London Airport in about four hours. Mid-week night flights, if less convenient, are substantially cheaper and well worth considering. The journey by rail and sea takes three exhausting days, works out at much the same price, and will interest only those with a rooted objection to flying, or those wishing to stop off frequently on the way. There are connections by boat and hydrofoil with Syracuse.

Within Malta there are two alternatives. Most of the more important sites are accessible by bus. Buses are extraordinarily cheap and run regularly to all the villages. But they are incredibly slow, and as all services operate from Valletta, one must be based there if they are to be a practical proposition. The self-drive hire car is more expensive (at present 30/– to 40/– a day) but is very much faster and more flexible for arranging a programme. Hire cars, distinguished by their yellow number plates, have a poor reputation for maintenance in the island, whether rightly or wrongly, and need watching. Consideration of other road users is not a prominent feature of Maltese driving either. Country roads can be narrow and tortuous, and some village streets are as bad. If the picture appears rather black, I can only say I have driven several thousand miles round Malta and Gozo, despite its small size, and have enjoyed most of them.

For anyone staying above a week, Gozo is a must. A ferry crosses several times daily from Marfa. If the weather is bad enough for it to use alternative landing places at Paradise Bay or St Paul's Bay, one might be wiser to stay in Malta. It will not need to get much worse before one runs the danger of being stranded indefinitely in Gozo. This, however, happens only very rarely in the summer months, and there are worse fates. In winter, the 1 p.m. return crossing is much more reliable than the 4 p.m. one. Cars are carried but have to be booked in advance, during the summer well in advance. For a day's visit, one of the fleet of taxis which meet the boat at Mġarr harbour is a simple, if rather more expensive, solution. A boat runs daily from Valletta, departing at noon, a slow but scenic voyage.

Maps of the islands published by the Directorate of Overseas Surveys are available from Edward Stanford Ltd, 12/14 Long Acre, London W.C.2, or the Office of Public Works, Valletta. Coverage is provided in three sheets at a stated price of 4/6 each, on a scale of 1:25,000 (4 cm. to 1 km.). They are excellent on roads, modern buildings and topography, but tend to be erratic when it comes to antiquities. A number are not even shown. Note in particular that Kunċizzjoni temple should be at 406732, the Ġgantija at 342896 and Ta' Marżiena at 316881. Grid as at 1962. Older maps have a bewildering variety of grids, two differing so slightly as to lead to much confusion. I have myself been accused of quoting a reference to a shipwreck site on dry land through just such a misunderstanding.

Malta is a boom island for tourism, though the pace of development has slackened somewhat since the easing of currency restrictions from Britain. The many new hotels opened and still opening have yet to acquire the character and individuality which the older ones have established over the years.

Just outside Valletta is the Phoenicia, an international hotel, with all that that implies. Inside the walls there are the Castille and three smaller and much more modest ones, the British, the Bellevue and the Osborne. With these should be mentioned the Melita at Balzan, at the gates of the San Anton Gardens. The Xara Palace, inside the walls of Mdina, has more grace and character than any, but is not cheap. The Duke of Edinburgh in Victoria, Gozo, is strong on character too, of the sort which over the years collects many anecdotes. It is reliably reported that its only bath was occupied one night by a large, live turtle, though it is only fair to mention that this was before extensive renovations and enlargements. I have myself had to summon help from the bottom of the garden to escape from a bedroom which had no door handle on the inner side.

The modern hotels fall into two groups. Most are at Sliema, the most anglicized part of the island, which one may consider advantage or disadvantage according to taste. Others are to be found placed strategically round the coasts, at St Paul's Bay, Golden Bay, Mellieħa Bay, Paradise Bay, Comino, Marsalforn, etc. A very large one is now being built at Rabat which, when complete, should have wonderful views of the island, despite its own deplorable effect on the Rabat skyline. The choice between the groups depends on one's preference for town or country, night life or beaches, activity or relaxation. Malta is so small that all parts are easily accessible from any centre on the main island. There is comparatively little to choose between the hotels within each group, of which in any case there will be several more by the time this is in print.

Maltese cooking is on the whole undistinguished. Italian and English menus are normally offered. A few local dishes are well worth enquiring for. Pastizzi, pasties of soft cheese in flaky pastry, go excellently with mid-morning coffee. Timpana, unkindly translated as 'paste pie' (baked macaroni under a pastry lid), can be very good, but is not to be recommended to anyone on a slimming diet. Stewed rabbit is a traditional dish, particularly at the open air feast of Mnarja in the Buskett Gardens, which the Maltese are unnecessarily modest about, the best I have tasted on the island. Fish, stewed in its own juice, can be memorable. Unfortunately the tastiest, the famed lampuki (coryphene), has only a very short season in late August and September.

The local wine deserves at the very least passing mention. The best hardly compares with the high quality wines of the Continent, but is more than adequate and remarkably cheap. I would never consider drinking an imported one. The wine served in the local bars varies considerably in quality, but at 6d the tumbler, 1/6 the bottle, mistakes are not expensive. It comes in three colours, red, white and amber. The last can easily be confused with whisky in appearance, and vice versa, as I know to my cost. It tends to be rather heavy at times. One local make has produced perhaps the classic euphemism to explain any sediment—'phenomenal living substance'.

As regards season, spring (March to May inclusive) and autumn (October) are undoubtedly best for seeing the sites. In summer temperatures, the pull of the sea is a constant temptation away from the archaeology, though the Hypogeum and the Catacombs retain their appeal throughout. In the winter months, the weather is naturally rather more erratic, but rarely bad for more than two or three days at a time.

Underground and indoor sites should be sufficient to fill profitably any but the longest spells of inclemency at any season.

Whatever the time of year, it is worth enquiring for any local feasts during the period of one's stay. Not that it is easy to overlook one, owing to the Maltese propensity for noisy fireworks. Church and street decorations, the processions, and the set-piece fireworks which round off all celebrations should be watched for in particular.

Finally, a very useful and helpful body for all or any problems or queries of oversea visitors to Malta is the Government Tourist Office, Valletta.

1 · THE HARBOUR AREA

VALLETTA

Any tour of Malta must begin with Valletta, which has been the capital of the island since it was founded by the Knights immediately after the Great Siege of 1565. The city was laid out on a generous grid plan, with noble buildings like the Conventual Church (now the Cathedral) of St John, the Palace of the Grand Masters, the Auberges or hostels of the Knights, one for each linguistic group, and, most impressive of all, the fortifications from St Elmo, scene of the bitterest fighting of the siege, to the land walls across the neck of the promontory.

This wealth of 16th to 20th century history in stone is not, however, the concern of this guide, and has meant the complete obliteration of signs of any earlier occupation. Before the building of St Elmo in 1552, the headland of Xiberras is said to have been devoid of buildings. This may well have been something of an exaggeration since quantities of medieval pottery and other rubbish have been found incorporated in the glacis before the walls. Cart-ruts came to light in the rock outside Kingsgate when new approach roads were being laid out between the wars, implying a settlement on the site of the later city as far back as the Bronze Age.

There is much to see within Valletta, but we must confine our attention to the Auberge de Provence, on the north side of Kingsway roughly half way between Kingsgate and Palace Square.

THE NATIONAL MUSEUM

The National Museum has been housed since 1958 in the Auberge de Provence in Kingsway, though there are plans for its return to the Auberge d'Italie in Merchant Street, its home from 1922 to 1942. The Auberge, designed by Girolamo Cassar, dates to 1571. The façade, entrance hall, and particularly the main hall on the first floor are worth examination in their own right. The archaeological collection is confined to the ground floor (Fig. 4), the mezzanine floor being occupied by the

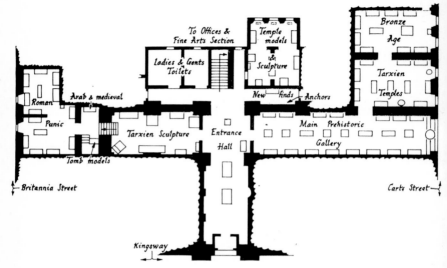

Fig. 4. The National Museum of Malta, the Archaeological Section

Museum Department offices and the first floor by the Fine Art Section.

In the *Entrance Hall* are relief models of the city of Valletta and of the whole island (a similar map of Gozo is in the Gozo Museum). Both are useful in picturing the topography, far more so than simple two-dimensional maps. Beyond the ticket desk, the *Main Gallery* opens to the right.

The showcases are in approximately chronological order, working along the right-hand wall first. With the prehistoric sequence already described, and the sites themselves to be dealt with individually later, all that is required here is a brief summary and a note of the more important or interesting pieces.

Case 1. Għar Dalam phase, represented from Għar Dalam (p. 81) and Skorba (p. 135). Typical Impressed Ware, closely related to that of the Stentinello Culture in Sicily. Date about 4000 B.C. (but see note on dates, p. 20).

Case 2. Grey and Red Skorba phases, from the type site. The forked handled ladles are very curious. The red trumpet lugs relate to the

Diana Ware of Sicily. Most intriguing of all are the female figurines in terracotta and stone (Fig. 5). The minute head with its upturned triangular face recalls examples from the Cyclades. The two cores of obsidian, for the production of knife-blades, were imports from Pantelleria and Lipari respectively. Obsidian is a natural glass much prized in antiquity. Its sources are few and the products of each are identifiable, yielding valuable evidence, as here, on the distribution pattern of ancient trade.

Fig. 5. Female figurine from Skorba, Red Skorba phase, *c.* 3300 B.C. Height 7 cm

Case 3. Żebbuġ phase, from five tombs discovered near that village in 1947. These appear to have been simple pits, unlike the later shaft-and-chamber tombs. Date about 3200 B.C. Note the stele with a rough human face. A group of representative sherds from domestic levels at Skorba is added. Here too one can see stylized human figures incorporated in the designs.

Case 4. Mġarr and Ġgantija. The Mġarr phase, being a short transitional one, is poorly represented. Its material is nowhere plentiful. The Mġarr temples (p. 137) are shown in a three-dimensional model on a central table. In the showcase, notice the little contemporary model of a temple building, carved in stone. Its rocf is of long transverse elements, possibly baulks of timber. The finds from the Ġgantija itself are mainly in the Gozo Museum. Of this site too there is a table model showing its appearance (p. 153). A tomb at Benġemma (p. 126) produced the

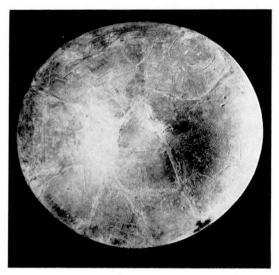

Plate 1. From the Hypogeum, the plate engraved with
bulls and goats (*above*)—diameter 25.5 cm.—and the
'Sleeping Lady' (*below*)—length 12.2 cm

elegant dishes of this phase on the lower shelf. The Ġgantija phase is much better represented in the Xemxija cases, next following.

Cases 5–7. Ġgantija phase, the Xemxija tombs (p. 143). Plans on the wall show the six shaft-and-chamber tombs. The cases contain a small proportion of their rich contents. There is great variety in the decoration of the pottery. Note too the axe amulets, of a hard greenstone imported from at nearest the toe of Italy.

Case 8. Mnajdra (p. 97). The table model shows the site, and the stone bowl on the steps the largest find from it. Being an old excavation, very little material has survived from it, but this includes the curious terracotta figurines and twists of clay, the significance of which escapes us.

Cases 9 and 10, centre case and table model. The Hypogeum of Ħal Saflieni (p. 58). This extraordinary temple-cemetery produced a remarkable wealth of pottery, personal ornaments and human bones. All are well represented here. Note in particular the circular plate with a scratched design of bulls and goats, and the Sleeping Lady, one of the most famous of Maltese prehistoric finds (Plate 1). This is a graceful little terracotta figurine, only 12·2 cm. long, showing a woman of generous proportions asleep on a couch. Her significance is discussed on p. 64. She is accompanied here by a variety of other figurines, including another sleeping woman of rather less elegance.

Cases 11 and 12, centre case and table model. Ħaġar Qim (p. 93). As at Mnajdra, the exhibits are mainly the result of recent small-scale excavation, necessitated by restoration work. Few of the finds from the clearance of the temple in 1847 have survived. Most notable are the figurines in the centre case, one standing frontally on a pitted pedestal, three seated with their knees bent sideways. All lack their heads, which the perforations suggest were made separately. In contrast to these corpulent but sexless figures, the naturalistic terracotta in the wall case should on no account be missed. She is sometimes, and fairly, referred to as the Venus of Malta. The arms are still somewhat stylized, but the modelling of the torso, the shoulders in particular, is masterly. It is sad that the head is missing.

Case 13, Xrobb il-Għaġin (p. 78) and Tal Qadi (p. 133), and *Case 14,* Kordin III (p. 57), add little of special note.

Plate 2. The seated 'goddess' from Ḥaġar Qim—height
23.5 cm

The *Tarxien Room* is devoted solely to the finds from the temples at
Tarxien, which have given their name to the last phase of the temple
period, 2400–2000 B.C. The pottery in the wall cases illustrates the
variety of decorative techniques now employed in addition to the final
development of the scratched ware. But in the stores, if not in the showcases, the stereotyped scratched volutes outnumber all other designs
many times over. The great bowls outside the cases demonstrate the
technical skill of the potters. The mirror fitted below one of them allows
the visitor to see the imprint of the fig leaves which lined the mould
supporting its lower wall. The pedestalled bowl (Fig. 6) in the case to
the left of the next doorway is a fine example of a type imported to
Malta, perhaps from Sicily but closely related to forms in the north
Aegean, at sites like Thermi and the Second City of Troy.

Fig. 6. Pedestal
bowl from Tarxien,
a foreign import.
Height 10 cm

This case also contains, like the two to its left, some of the stonework from the temples—querns, hammerstones, the unique two-man stone-dressing axe. The domed conical objects are of unknown use, their resemblance to Etruscan gravestones surely accidental. Smaller tools of chert (a local poor form of flint), flint (from Sicily) and obsidian (from Lipari) are shown in one of the table cases, together with various small ornaments. The only metal discovered at this level was the gold inlay in a stone bead displayed here. Note the peculiar slip of bone with oval bosses carved on it, a poor example of a fascinating class of object, again of unknown use, found in south-east Sicily, the heel of Italy, southern Greece and Troy.

It remains to refer to the figurines, once more singling out only a few of the more noteworthy. In the centre case nearest the window, the figures are closely related to those from Ħaġar Qim, if in rather different postures. The 'stools' on which two are seated have diminutive relief figures on the sides. The clay figure in the wall case next to the door is often described as 'the priest', though there is no clear basis for this identification. It was modelled on a straw core, the imprint of which can still be seen.

The last centre case is worth lingering over, as many of its diminutive figures repay close examination. One is a gross object with its body stuck full of sharp flints, suggesting black magic. By contrast, another is a seductive creature, sensitively modelled in clay and less than 4 centimetres high. Several heads carved from stone are even smaller. The carved phalli are important evidence on the religious beliefs of the builders (see also p. 25).

Bronze Age Room. The next room holds material from the succeeding Bronze Age. The temple civilization collapsed about 2000 B.C. for reasons we can only guess at, and was succeeded by a culture at a lower level, showing absolutely no sign of continuity with the old. It looks a clear case of foreign invasion. Most of the temples were abandoned and the rest were adapted to other uses. Tarxien itself became a cemetery, and the rows of complete bowls (Fig. 7) and jars displayed here, remarkably different from those of the temple period, were found deposited with the cremated ashes of the dead. Similar pottery occurs at this period over much of the Central Mediterranean and in Western Greece, but more work is needed on the nature and date of its distribution.

As so often with burials, the deceased took with them to the tomb

Fig. 7. Decorated bowl from the Tarxien
Cemetery, first half of the second
millennium B.C. Diameter 13 cm

some of their personal possessions and ornaments. The bronze axes and
flat daggers show that certainly by now metal was coming into the
island. The beads of faience too are imports—plentiful ones as the 6,000
from one jar show. Fish bones make attractive beads as well. Figurines
still occur, on the top shelf of the centre case, but of a completely new
form. A fairly naturalistic one has an imposing and beautifully modelled
headdress. Others, however, are stylized to a mere disc with feet and
simple knob head.

The table model shows the temples as they appear today. The later
burials were found in the fill above the floors of the Southern Temple.

The remaining four wall cases illustrate the later phases of pre-
historic Malta, named after the sites of Borġ in-Nadur (p. 82) and
Baħrija (p. 124). The former, running from about 1400 to about 800
B.C., is characterized by red-slipped pottery, particularly a pedestalled
bowl and a cup with a T-shaped projection from the top of its handle.
One small sherd is of especial importance, testifying to contact with the
Mycenaeans of Late Bronze Age Greece. It is from the lip of a well-
known type of Mycenaean drinking goblet.

The Baħrija phase was shorter, and overlapped the end of the Borġ
in-Nadur phase. Its material is restricted to a few sites only. It is black-
slipped, with cut-out meander designs, and has connections with
Southern Italy in the Iron Age. The anchor-shaped objects of pottery
probably served in some form of loom.

From here one must retrace one's steps to the Entrance Hall, where
one turns to the right into the *New Finds Corridor*. A case on the left
allows the display of the most recently discovered material, supple-
mented by drawings and photographs on the wall boards on either side.

Details cannot, naturally, be given here as the display is frequently altered to keep pace with further finds as they are made.

Also on show here is some of the material recovered from the sea-bed around Malta, particularly the lead stocks and collars of Roman anchors. A reconstruction is given on p. 151. The largest is a monstrous stock weighing over 3 tons, brought up with some difficulty from off Buġibba. All have been discovered and lifted by aqualung divers over the last ten years or so.

The *Temple Models and Sculpture Room* serves two functions, as its name implies. The wall cases house smaller pieces of carved stonework from the temples. The two large triangular objects, from Mġarr and Tarxien, may be stone anchors, votive offerings in the temples. The biconical ones resemble slingstones, though they would be abnormally large for this purpose. The second case has a fascinating collection of architectural models on various scales, contemporary with the buildings they depict. It is not clear whether we should regard them again as votive offerings, or as architects' models. They come from various sites, Tarxien in particular.

The fragments of the façade model are invaluable in any reconstruction of the temples' original appearance (p. 28). The lower right corner piece can be matched in every particular from the still existing remains— as at Ħaġar Qim for example. The upper left corner can surely, then, be accepted as accurate, though its details have nowhere survived. The 'ground plan' model, with an agglomeration of rectangular rooms on a low podium, is more problematical. If it was an architect's design piece, nothing remains in Malta to suggest it was ever built.

The rest of the room is devoted to carved blocks of larger size, from Buġibba (the fish and spirals), Ħaġar Qim (double spirals), Xrobb il-Għaġin (pitting) and Tarxien (the block with pitting on one face, then turned to the wall to be redecorated with a curvilinear motif on what had been its back). But pride of place goes to the elegantly designed altar from Ħaġar Qim (Fig. 8) and the 'fat lady' in relief from Tas-Silġ.

Beyond the Entrance Hall, the *Tarxien Sculpture Room* contains more of the carved blocks from that site. All are described in more detail from the modern copies which have replaced them on the site (pp. 68, 69). The great statue is our clearest record of the divinity of the temples. It is more than unfortunate that time and the local farmers have reduced her to waist level. The block opposite shows even more

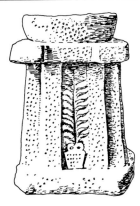

Fig. 8. Decorated altar from Ħaġar Qim. Height 73 cm

clearly the replacement of pitting by relief spirals. The altar in the far corner contained strong evidence, circumstantial it is true, for animal sacrifice, in the shape of many bones inside the niche above, and a long flint knife blade and goat-horn core behind the D-shaped plug in its front.

The spiral decoration calls for a further word. This used to be attributed to influence from Mycenae in the 17th century B.C. As radiocarbon dates pushed the temples back in time, so earlier sources had to be suggested, first Minoan Crete, then Middle Kingdom Egypt. But with the recent revision of radiocarbon chronologies, even these can no longer be supported, and the argument for development within the island, as with the temples themselves, becomes correspondingly stronger.

At the top of the steps, a case on the left has scale models of Punic and Roman tombs (Fig. 9). There is a chronological sequence from the round-shaft:oval-chamber form, starting back in the temple period, through the square-shaft:transverse-rectangular-chamber, to the rectangular-chamber-and-shaft-in-line, which came in during the Roman occupation. The large square pit is an exceptional form, the catacomb being more typical of the later Roman period. The case on the right falls for consideration below.

The *Punic Room.* From this point, about the 9th century B.C., Malta's isolation breaks down and it becomes part of a larger state, firstly the trading empire of the Phoenicians and subsequently that of

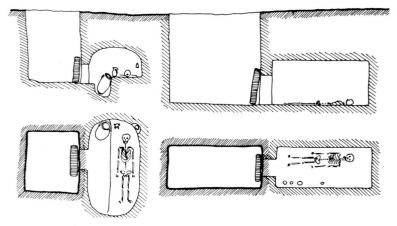

Fig. 9. Plans of typical Punic (*left*) and Roman (*right*) tombs

Carthage. Our evidence comes almost solely from the tombs, the contents of a few of which are displayed. More are to be seen in the Roman Villa Museum at Rabat, p. 109.

Even where not themselves imports, like the Corinthian 8th century cup and Rhodian 7th century bird bowl from Għajn Qajjet, and on the other side of the doorway the Campanian jugs from 3rd to 2nd century Italy, these vessels belong to a foreign tradition. They are all, for a start, wheel made. Their close relatives are to be looked for in the cities of Phoenicia and North Africa. Work on their connections and dating still has a long way to go. The great terracotta coffin in the centre is certainly Phoenician work, but of Egyptian inspiration. The resemblance to a mummy case is no accident.

The stone pillar is a votive *cippus* from Marsaxlokk (? Tas-Silġ), one of a pair of which the other is in the Louvre. Its inscriptions in Greek and Phoenician helped in the decipherment of the latter language.

The *Roman Room*. At the centre stands another terracotta coffin, this time copying a wooden chest. The case in the window holds more Punic inscriptions, from Rabat, Ħal Far and Gozo.

The other cases are of more tomb groups, of the period after Malta had passed to Rome in 218 B.C. However, it is immediately obvious that there was a considerable cultural overlap, and many of the pieces are still Punic rather than Roman. Part of the overlap is accidental, since many of the tombs were repeatedly reopened to add further burials. The tomb from Hamrun, for example, contained all three types of lamp, the Punic *bilychnis* saucer with pinched lip, the closed early Roman lamp, and the later Romano-Maltese lamp without decoration or handle. Imported pottery is less in evidence, though there is a fine 2nd century B.C. bowl of Megaran manufacture from Tarxien. The glass-ware, particularly the fine bowl from Qrendi, is worthy of note.

The last chapter of Maltese archaeology is represented, though very poorly it must be admitted, in the case at the head of the steps on return. The curious vessels on the upper shelves, mainly water jars and lamps, betray strong North African influence. Though not closely datable, they must belong to a style introduced by the Arabs when Malta was ruled from Tunisia, A.D. 870–1090. The sherds of glazed bowls on the lower shelves conversely mirror the recovery of the island by Europe and Christianity, being of Sicilian and Italian origin. But the African tradition took long to die. *Mnara* lamp holders betraying its influence were still being made at the beginning of this century.

The *Coin Room*. Finally the coin collection, housed in a room on the first floor, can be visited by application to the staff. Here the main interest, in the present context, lies in the first small case. It contains examples of the few coins minted in the islands for local use in Punic times. They bear inscriptions in Greek, Phoenician or both, ΜΕΛΙΤΑΕΑ and ΓΑVΛΙΤΟΝ, Malta and Gozo. Punic trade brought coins from the cities of Sidon and Aradus in Phoenicia, from Cathage itself of course, and from a number of the cities of Greece and its western colonies.

The collections of Roman and Byzantine coinage is of little more than local interest. For the later periods, the coins record the successive dynasties which held the islands, Arab, Norman, Swabian, Angevin, Aragonese and Castilian. The issues of the Knights and of the British are far fuller and, particularly the former, of more interest to the numismatist, but fall outside the limits of an archaeological guide.

THE FORTIFICATIONS

Although not strictly within our scope, an exception must be made to allow a further word on the fortifications of the island. They are easily

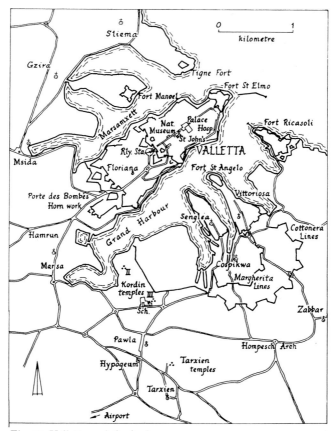

Fig. 10. Valletta and the harbour area

the most impressive in Europe to survive from the 16th to 18th centuries, the peak period of military architecture (Fig. 10).

Fort St Elmo, at the tip of the Valletta peninsula, was built by the Knights to control the harbour mouth in 1552. It started as a star-shaped fort but has many later additions. The latest were the concrete 6-pounder towers of 1940, which saw action in the Italian E-boat raid of 25th July 1941.

The main inland defences of La Vallette's city are the great walls and dry moat originally pierced only at Kingsgate and at the two ends.

Besides the additional entrance at the Castille, Kingsgate itself has recently been substantially enlarged. Notice below the bridge to the south where the Malta Railway crossed the moat to its underground Valletta terminus, a precious fragment of industrial archaeology. The towers or cavaliers of St James and St John added further to the strength of the defence. Outside the walls, a broad strip of land was kept bare as a field of fire.

In the later 17th century, an outer defence was built to take in the growing suburb of Floriana, together with the granary pits in front of the church of St Publius. These walls too had a main central entrance at the Porte des Bombes. The gate itself originally spanned the gap in the wall near the present roundabout, and was moved a hundred metres or so downhill to ease the traffic congestion at this point. The approach was further overlooked by the Horn Work, which projects from the Floriana walls to the south of the main road. The whole of the area now covered by gardens, cemeteries, petrol stations, and the like was kept as another open glacis before the walls. Below ground, a maze of tunnels was cut to protect the walls from hostile mining.

The defences of the Three Cities, east of Grand Harbour, have a similar history (Plate 3). The nucleus of the defence is Fort St Angelo, dating to the period before the Knights came to Malta. It was Vallette's headquarters through the siege. The walls of Vittoriosa and Senglea were the ones which withstood the Turks in 1565, though they needed very substantial rebuilding after the rough treatment they received that summer. In 1638 the Margherita Lines were thrown round the developing suburb of Cospicua. Later still, the Cottoner brothers, successive Grand Masters of the Order, began the Cottonera Lines in 1670 to take in a wider area. Finally, the wall enclosing the military area on the Corradino (Kordin) Heights was added, not being completed until after the British came to Malta.

The Knights' hold on the harbour area was completed by Forts Ricasoli, Manoel and Tigne on the promontories around it in the later 17th and 18th centuries.

The walls of Mdina (p. 104) and the Gran Castello of Gozo (p. 148) will be referred to later, as will the Victoria Lines across north Malta (p. 127). The watchtowers and occasional larger forts commanding each possible invasion beach or inlet are a conspicuous feature of the coasta scenery.

It is easy to dismiss the colossal expenditure of money and effort on these walls, even if largely provided by slave labour, as a complete

Plate 3. Grand Harbour, Valletta, the entrance and Fort Ricasoli (*above*), and the walls of Senglea and the dockyard (*below*). The occasion is the regatta held on 8th September to commemorate the raising of the siege in 1565

waste. They were surrendered to the French without a blow in 1798, and though the French defended Valletta against the Maltese and English for two years, the other walls never had a shot fired against them until the aerial bombardments of 1941. But, for a century or more after 1565, the threat of another Moslem attack was a very real one. That it never came may be taken as proof that the walls were a success rather than as evidence of their failure—their strength was enough in itself to discourage attack.

THE HARBOUR AREA

The intensity of occupation around the whole harbour area has been nearly as great as that within Valletta itself. It is remarkable that any antiquities have surved here at all.

West of Marsamxett, the heights of Mensija have produced traces of prehistoric occupation in the form of sherds and cart-ruts, and there are remains of a Roman round tower at Ta' Ċieda, on the outskirts of L'Imsieraħ, but these are hardly worth searching out. East of Grand Harbour, in the Three Cities area the dearth is even greater. Nothing survives to support the tradition of a classical temple on the promontory of Bighi, in contrast to the discoveries at Tas-Silġ (p. 78), which now has much the better claim to identification with the Temple of Juno. The ancient use of the harbours can hardly be doubted, but the only direct evidence we can point to is the discovery from time to time of Roman masonry along Stables Street, on the northern side of the Marsa sports ground. Here stood quays and warehouses, part of the port facilities when the Marsa creek extended further inland than it does today.

But indirect evidence of Punic and Roman interest in the area is plentiful, in the form of tombs, singly and in groups, from Msida in the west to Żabbar in the east, but particularly at Tal Ħorr and Għajn Dwieli, on either side of Pawla. If we find nothing above ground, it is not because it was never there but because it has been obliterated since.

This interest did not begin with the Phoenicians. A cluster of pre-historic sites within a kilometre or so of the head of the harbour, including two of the islands' most important ones, shows that it began much earlier.

KORDIN

Closest to the harbour are three groups of ruins on the Corradino or Kordin Heights. Time and air bombardment in 1941 have dealt harshly with two of them, so that visits, as well as being difficult (one is on service property), are hardly worth while. The third, Kordin III, is in much better shape. It is in a walled enclosure (key at the National Museum) in the north-east corner of the grounds of the Government Technical School on the Marsa–Cospicua road. The gate is to the rear, planned before the school was thought of, and opens on to the back of the monument.

The site is a trefoil temple of early type, the sherds beneath its floors and forecourt placing it firmly in the Ġgantija phase. The cobbled court nestles into a typical concave façade, though the walls are now very much reduced. The entrance gives on to a central court very similar to that at Mġarr, with three large apses all more or less separated off. The screening walls were probably all additions in the Tarxien phase, as documented at Skorba. As with the other early temples, there are no traces of decorated blocks—the keynote is simplicity.

There is, however, one very notable feature, namely the 2·75 metre long recumbent slab at the inner left corner of the court. In its surface are seven deep transverse grooves, obviously produced by grinding. If the date of the grooves could be established, the choice between the two likeliest interpretations would be easy. One view would place them in the temple period, and make them querns, or rather a communal multiple quern. The corn for the community would be ground within the temple of, and so under the protection of, the goddess. The second view suggests that they are as recent as the 18th or 19th centuries A.D., the result of grinding up prehistoric potsherds to turn into *deffun*, the traditional Maltese roofing material before the introduction of modern cements. All one can say for certain is that their present appearance dated from before the excavation in 1908 by Peet and Ashby of the British School at Rome.

Behind the temple are many small, irregular and comparatively slightly built rooms, as at Ħaġar Qim and Mnajdra. They are contemporary with the temple and probably associated with it, as store-rooms and the like. They do not appear to be one of the still missing temple period settlements. However, excavation beneath them has shown that there was occupation on the site before the temple was built, paralleling the cases of Skorba and Mġarr.

Kordin III, in short, is a pleasant little site, but hardly one the short-term visitor need bother with. Apart from the unique grindstone, it shows nothing which cannot be seen better elsewhere.

THE HYPOGEUM

By contrast, the Hypogeum is in every way unique. It is a kilometre south of the Kordin site, barely 100 metres south of Pawla Square and in the angle between the Luqa and Marsa roads, in the district known as Ħal Saflieni. The entrance is in Hypogeum Street, on the further, south, side of the first block.

It is an unpromising district for ancient remains, which adds to the impact it makes on visitors. It was discovered in the course of housing development in 1902, when workmen cutting cisterns for the new houses broke through its roof. Unfortunately, the knowledge of it was deliberately hushed up until the houses were complete, by which time considerable and avoidable further damage had been done to the upper levels. The next chapter of its story is little more cheerful. Investigation of the site was entrusted to Father Magri, S.J., who cleared the central chambers but then left for missionary work in the East. Though most of his finds were preserved, no record of their context or associations survives.

The work was completed in a much more scientific manner by Dr Zammit in 1905–9. Subsequently the site was prepared for visitors by cutting a more convenient direct approach to the middle floor, and by installing lighting. With the National Museum and the Tarxien Temples, the Hypogeum is one of the three sites which no visitor to Malta, however short his stay, can afford to miss.

Both the external and internal doorways at the entrance are modelled on temple trilithons. A few showcases of representative material and casts of some of the more important pieces (originals in Valletta, p. 45) give some introduction. The scale model of the site is more helpful to an understanding of its complexity than any two-dimensional plan. The modern stair well, cut through the rock, carries one down 4 metres, whence a passage leads, via the bottom of the cistern which disclosed the cavities, direct to the heart of the site, some 5·25 metres below the modern surface (Fig. 11). The original entrance, a more logical point to start a description of the layout, is up two flights of steps to the right of the central 'lobby'.

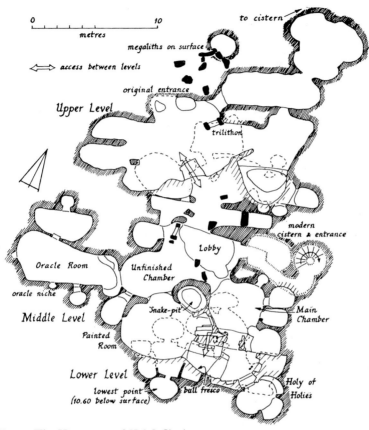

Fig. 11. The Hypogeum of Ħal Saflieni

Here, through a hole in the house wall, one can see the papered walls of an Edwardian front parlour, and the inside of the front door opening on the street. The floor has been removed and cleared to the rock surface, on which stand a few scattered boulders. These are all that remains of a megalithic building, probably a temple but much too far gone for anything further to be said. North of the megaliths, and now accessible only by a tortuous route beneath the house foundations, a circular cistern was cut to provide the site with its water supply. It is 8 metres deep and roughly bell-shaped. Three ribs are left in the walls, as if supporting a corbelled dome, and these, together with the free use of ochre on the walls, confirm that it is contemporary with the monument. Its contents on excavation were very mixed, since it remained open and in use long after all access to the rest of the site was blocked.

On the other side of the megaliths, now separated from them by a house foundation wall, rough steps can be seen in the rock, leading into the first chamber, its floor already 2·75 metres below street level. There is a strong resemblance here to the tombs of Xemxija, p. 143, particularly in the lobed plan. We shall return to the probable significance of this shortly. A built trilithon stands to one side and other chambers, of similarly rough appearance, open off to left and right of it. The roughness is such that one cannot now be sure which rooms are natural caves in the rock, which are artificially enlarged, and which entirely man-made. What is certain, not only from logic but from the archaeological evidence, is that this is the oldest part of the site. Only when this area was found inadequate did the builders open up the chambers which form the middle stage.

The first group of chambers at this lower level is little different in technique, but, by lying that much deeper, has its ceilings almost intact. The room on the right at the foot of the steps has some of its original deposit returned to it after sorting, to give visitors some idea of the appearance of the site on discovery. The next steps bring one back to the point of modern entry. Immediately on the right, a built trilithon has been added to a hewn chamber, as if to tidy up the entrance after a change to a more sophisticated taste in architecture. An upright on the opposite side of the lobby was originally part of another trilithon leading to what, from its lavish treatment, must be considered the most important room.

This *Main Chamber* is roughly circular and carefully carved from the rock to give the impression of built masonry in the typical upright-and-lintel construction of the temples. A number of trilithon openings are represented, some blind, some leading to smaller chambers in the walls. The encroaching lintel just below ceiling level to the right strongly recalls the oversailing courses in the temples above ground. The effect of all this is heightened by the use of colour. Most of the wall surface, especially in the blank wall panels, has received a red wash of ochre. High on the right-hand wall is a patch of painted black and white chequers. It was from this room that the two 'sleeping lady' figurines were recovered. The floor is 5·50 metres below surface.

The last opening from the central Lobby is a broad one of very unfinished appearance. The wall is deeply pitted, suggesting the technique of excavation. Holes were pecked or drilled and the rock then prised out and removed. The surface would then have been dressed smooth with mauls, though this stage had been omitted here. Some ochre, however, had already been applied.

From the end of this room, steps lead down into the so-called *Oracle Room*. It is roughly rectangular, with three oval side-chambers of various sizes. The smallest, at face level in the left-hand wall, has the peculiarity of producing a powerful echo or reverberation to a deep voice. A good deal has been said and written about the acoustical skill of the builders to produce this effect, by means of the moulding at ceiling level in the end wall of the room it has been suggested. Short of testing this by the drastic means of cutting away the moulding, it is probably safer to regard the echo as quite accidental. Less marked effects of the same kind can be found elsewhere, in the Holy of Holies for example. This is not to deny that its suitability for religious ceremonies may not have been recognized and exploited to the full. The effect is certainly eerie, even today under full electric light.

The Oracle Room is further distinguished by having an elaborately painted ceiling. Sweeping, if rather inconsequential, spirals have been added in red ochre, with circular blobs here and there. There is none of the competence and skill of the stone relief spirals in the temples, but we may here be looking at the first doodlings of wall decoration, which led on to the reliefs at a later stage. What we cannot know is whether patterns appeared on the wall plaster which once covered the insides of many, if not all, of the temples.

The next room to be considered, also leading out of the Unfinished Chamber, has another painted vault, though the designs here, on the ceiling at least, tend to be smaller, fussier and less well preserved. There is a good row of spirals within honeycomb compartments on the upper walls.

Three openings in the left-hand wall open respectively into a side niche, the Main Chamber and the innermost part of the site. The niche has provision for a screen across its entrance, and its floor opens directly into a 2 metre deep pit with concave walls and a sloping shelf around it. It would certainly serve admirably for either keeping snakes or collecting alms, both of which have been suggested. In the absence of anything remotely like proof, visitors may care to add their own conjectures. The two flanking pillars bear pitted and ochred decoration, another temple feature. The stepped floor of the second opening is built rather than carved, and forms the roof of a stair passage.

The third opening leads into a sort of antechamber of extraordinary interest. On its left are the stairs to the lowest storey, the central niche of the Main Chamber, and a lower, somewhat damaged, side niche. At the end on the right is the magnificent carved façade of the so-called *Holy of Holies* (Plate 4). This consists of a 'porthole' slab under the centre of a lintel supported by four uprights. This is in turn framed

Plate 4. The Holy of Holies in the Hypogeum of Ħal Saflieni

within a larger trilithon and topped by another course of corbelling before the flat ceiling. But these details are not built but carved with meticulous care from the living rock. The fine tooling can be made out on any surface on which the light falls obliquely. In the floor is a large V-perforation, here surely for libation offerings rather than for tethering, its openings closable with stone plugs cut for the purpose.

The chamber within hardly seems to warrant this care and attention. It is so rough as to suggest that it may have been in the course of enlargement at the time of abandonment. In particular, a pilaster appears to be in process of being cut away. But even the surfaces not yet cut into appear nothing out of the ordinary. For the focal point of this whole extraordinary site, this small room, to say the least, is puzzling.

Before descending the stairs to the *Lower Storey*, visitors should pause to look at the wall opposite them. Dark lines of black paint outline what is apparently intended as a bull. It is crudely done, and the head and shoulders have not survived. That it is ancient and intentional is shown by the fact that the ochre wash on the wall ceases exactly at the black line. The bulls in relief at Tarxien (p. 72) offer parallels.

The lintel over the steps is one of the few cut blocks on the site, let into a groove in the rock cut carefully to receive it. The lower steps, too, are separate blocks, and distinctly irregular, though hardly sufficiently so to warrant the suggestion that they were intended to trip uninvited intruders. They lead into a maze of chambers, separated by septal walls as much as 1·70 metres above their floors. The present gangway and handrail are entirely modern additions. The innermost room has four side niches, the one on the left being the deepest point of the site, 10·60 metres below the surface. Note here another curved pilaster, and the way in which natural fissures in the rock have been used to help in the original cutting. There is free use of an ochre wash over many of the walls.

It is now time to consider the overall function of this intriguing site. For a start, the name gives away nothing. It is merely an archaeological label for any cavity below the ground, with the implication that ignorance forbids us to be more specific. As we have seen in our general consideration of the temples, it is easy to pursue the evidence so far, but impossible to take it further except by unsubstantiated guesswork. The evidence first. The decorated chambers must surely from their appearance be a temple. Indeed, they seem to be deliberate copies of the temples built above ground, particularly in the trilithon construction and the use of corbelling—both quite inappropriate to rock-cut chambers.

But the contents of the side chambers at the time of excavation equally clearly indicate burial. Zammit calculated from a careful count of the human bones in one surviving area that between 6,000 and 7,000 individuals, together with a wealth of personal ornaments, amulets and pottery offerings, had been buried down here. They lay principally in the side niches, and though some had spilled into the central chambers, these could be considered late and accidental encroachment into the 'cemetery chapel'. This is the part of the site, however, which Magri cleared, with no record of exactly what was found where.

The lower storey contained no bones or offerings, only water. It strongly suggests storage, perhaps, in view of those high dividing walls, of something which could be walked on, such as grain.

Beyond this, all is guesswork. The Sleeping Ladies look as if they are telling us something, but what? Are they seeking omens in dreams, or cures from illnesses by sleeping in a holy place? Could they be already dead? Are they worshippers, priestesses or the goddess herself? One cannot even be sure that one's guesses come anywhere near to exhausting the possibilities, or conversely that they necessarily exclude each other. What is implied is that the divinity is the same as that of the built temples, but that this divinity is here, quite naturally below ground, more concerned with death than with fertility.

What appears to have started as a simple rock-cut tomb became elaborated to include a funerary chapel at its heart. The similarities with the Roman catacombs at Rabat may not be accidental. If we leave aside what we know of the religion of the latter, there seems to be only a single firm contrast between the two sites—where the catacombs are rectilinear throughout, the Hypogeum is universally curvilinear, without a truly straight line anywhere.

But if the practices and beliefs of the place must for ever elude us, there are still a few valid implications to be drawn. Firstly, by being carved below ground, the Hypogeum has escaped destruction by the elements far better than any surface site. It is thus able to show us the high quality of surface finish in stone dressing (and in the Unfinished Room an intermediate stage in the process), the extensive use of colour in interior decoration, both as flat wash and in pattern, and the application of corbelling, or at least projecting courses, to the problem of roofing.

Secondly, the vast number of skeletons and the labour involved in its cutting need not stagger us. If Malta in this period supported a population of the order of 10,000, as suggested on p. 19, 7,000 burials could be made in two-thirds of an average life-span, 40 years at the outside. Yet the pottery found here shows that the life of the site covered from at least the Mġarr phase into early Tarxien, on present estimates 2900–2300 B.C. A lot of rock could be chipped out, and a lot of people could die, in six centuries. Perhaps, a tantalizing thought, there could be as many as fourteen other Hypogeums up and down the islands awaiting discovery.

TARXIEN

The Tarxien Temples lie 400 metres to the east of the Hypogeum. One should return towards Pawla Square, turn right at the main crossroads before the square, and watch for a signpost to the left just after the beginning of the one-way-street system. There is an unmistakably archaeological car-park provided, as neo-megalithic as the Hypogeum entrance, but with knobs on.

The custodian's house contains a small display collection. The cases duplicate what is more fully shown in the National Museum. More interesting are the carved blocks brought in from the site for protection from weathering, replaced by faithful modern copies in stone. The larger pieces we have already seen in Valletta (p. 49), but there is plenty of interest in the smaller ones here: the precision of the spiral-decorated screens on the end wall to the right, the smaller brambly block beside the door and the two animal processions, 22 sheep on one, two sheep, a ram(?) and a pig on the other, at the opposite end of the room.

On this wall, too, is a schematic painting of the stratigraphy over the site at the time of its excavation. It was discovered in 1914 when word of the farmer's troubles with great blocks of stone in his fields reached Dr Zammit. His first trenches in 1915 descended into the front apses of the South Temple, making dramatic discoveries immediately. Beneath modern disturbance, he came first on a cemetery layer with numerous cremated burials in small jars and bowls, with which were associated bronze weapons. These were dug into the top of a 60–90 cm. layer of sterile silt, beneath which was the rubbish, and more importantly the structure, of the temple. His work continued until the site was completely cleared by 1917. Even more than the Hypogeum 10 years before, Zammit's field notebooks give an admirable record of his excavation.

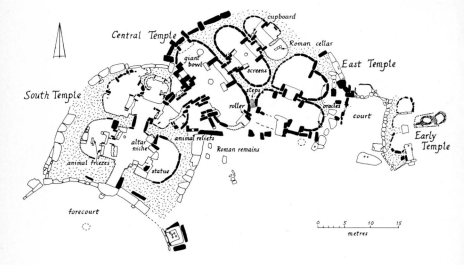

Central Temple

cupboard

Roman cellar

giant bowl

screens

East Temple

steps

South Temple

roller

oracles

court

Early Temple

altar niche

animal reliefs

Roman remains

animal friezes

statue

forecourt

0   5   10   15
metres

Fig. 12. The Tarxien Temples

His results were published in the Annual Report of the Museum year by year, and brought together in his book *Prehistoric Malta* in 1930.

The temples are now set in gardens, forming a little oasis in the modern housing estates. One enters first the great forecourt of the *South Temple* (Fig. 12), bounded by its concave façade and with a cistern, assumed to belong with the temple, at its centre. The spherical stones nearby are not cannonballs but rollers for manœuvring the great blocks, the earliest recorded use of ball-bearings. A good example will be noted in the second temple. The façade itself hardly survived above ground level, and to picture its original appearance one must combine in imagination the better-preserved façade of Ħaġar Qim and the contemporary relief model found on this site and now in Valletta.

There are two subsidiary structures, placed on the 'horns' of the façade, the right-hand one being the more complete. It consists of a horizontal slab roughly 3 metres square within a built frame. Its surface is hollowed and pierced by five holes, providing another fruitful source of speculation. Divination, gambling, or just amusement is always possible, with pebbles thrown to see which hole they fall into. However, libation is on the whole much likelier. Similar holes, often singly, can be found in other temples, notably Skorba and the Ġgantija, where the collection and draining away of liquid offerings seems the best explanation.

The V-perforation in a block in front of the main threshold slab may have served the same purpose, though the alternative of a tethering place for an animal awaiting sacrifice cannot be excluded. Ḣaġar Qim has a very similar feature in the same relative position.

The main entrance is modern restoration, part of the work financed by the Carnegie Corporation in 1956. Many other examples will be seen where cracked blocks have been capped with concrete partly to improve the appearance of the site but primarily to prevent rain water from seeping in to decay the stone. In no case can restoration and original be confused. Where the former height of a block is unknown,

Plate 5. The South Temple, Tarxien: the giant statue of the goddess

the top of the replacement has been left with a sinuous edge to indicate this. The front door is the sole exception. Its capstone is purely 'cosmetic' and its height above the ground an estimate. The proportions of doorways and passages, where recoverable, prove to follow a simple formula, from which it was easy to calculate a height, given only a width as here.

This temple is a good example of the 4-apse plan (p. 25), and dates to early in the Tarxien phase, by conventional C^{14} dates around 2400 B.C. The first court is beautifully paved and the most highly decorated of any in the temples.

One must respectfully start with the statue round the corner to the right (Plate 5). Whatever doubts there may be about the figurines, this must surely, from its size and position, be the goddess herself. When complete, she stood about 2.75 metres high, but time, weather, and above all the local farmers have reduced her to waist height. The slots for the wedges by which she was broken up for removal are clearly apparent on the original in Valletta. She wears a very full pleated skirt. It would be ungentlemanly to quote her hip measurements, and her calves are in proportion. She is supported, however, on small, elegant, but seriously overworked feet.

Her pedestal and the blocks on either side are decorated with various curvilinear repeat patterns. That to the right suggests an impressionistic view of a herd of cattle, though we cannot be sure that its carvers had the same imagery in mind. The rear of this apse, the line of which is well preserved, is strangely bare.

Between the orthostats and the passage to the inner court are two fine altar blocks, both with delicately carved running spirals. That to the right (Plate 6) still has a complete altar niche above, consisting of a typical 'porthole' slab, a rectangular flat slab on edge pierced by a rectangular hole, framed within a trilithon. The space behind was filled with animal bones on excavation. Even more dramatic was the discovery in the cavity in the block itself, referred to on p. 50. The flint knife blade must surely point to animal sacrifice on this block, the goat horn being from one of the victims. The niche above the left-hand altar is missing.

The western apse is also screened by decorated blocks, leaving a passage at its centre, beside which stands a stone bowl with pitted decoration. The orthostats forming the right-hand side of the passage bear scratches on their face which show well only in a cross light. They would seem to represent a series of simple boats. Such graffiti are quite

Plate 6. The South Temple, Tarxien: the altar niche which contained the sacrificial knife

common in later periods in Malta (see p. 86) but unique for the temple period. This disproves nothing, but when one sees the level to which the neighbouring walls have been destroyed (the small-stone rubble is modern restoration), one realizes that certainty of a prehistoric date for the designs is not possible. In any case, they are too schematic to tell us much. Certainly of the temple period are the decorated blocks around, in particular the two animal friezes (p. 65), now replaced by modern copies.

Because of the natural slope of the ground, preservation is progressively better as one moves inward. The next passage lacks only its lintels. Note the various V-perforations and bar-holes in the uprights. Both the passage and the next court are completely paved. It was the raising of this pavement which preserved a narrow border of the earlier pitted decoration on the great spiralled slab which separates the court from the terminal niche. This niche has opposed semicircular benches, which may have suggested the development of a third pair of side apses

in the next temple. These benches, too, are decorated. Notice the
arcaded effect of the relief design on the uprights on either side.

The apses to east and west of the inner court are both somewhat
irregular. The break in the temple's outer wall, allowing exit from the
left apse, is modern. Nestled in the angle behind the central niche is a
side shrine which shows some of the earlier fashion of pitted decoration.
The right-hand apse has been drastically altered to serve as entrance
passage to the second temple. Another porthole slab screens a small
chamber, the original inner end of the apse.

The Second or Central Temple is both bigger (23 metres long
internally), better preserved and finer structurally, but has much less
relief carving. It was inserted into the gap between the South and East
Temples in the full Tarxien period, somewhere after 2400 B.C. This
may explain why its axis falls outside the south-east quadrant normally
preferred by the temples. Although there was earlier occupation on the
site, the former view that at least the inner apses stood on the site of an
earlier temple can no longer be supported.

It is unique among surviving temples in having three pairs of apses
instead of the usual two. This may be considered a comparatively
minor elaboration of the 4-apse plan, already foreshadowed, indeed, by
the central niche of the South Temple. The further enlargement of the
stone paving to cover the whole of the first court and apses could be
regarded in the same light, as the extension of an already established
principle.

The entry passage from the South Temple (Plate 7), is amply provided
with V-perforations and bar-holes, and could obviously be secured
against unwanted visitors. The central court though less decorated
than that of the first temple, is even more impressive. The massive
stone paving and the closely fitting wall slabs give a powerful sense of
solidity. The widespread reddening of the stone here is not due to red
ochre, as in the Hypogeum, but to fire at the end of the temple period.
The quantities of fuel implied point to a heavy combustible roof—
beams, brush-wood and the like.

At the centre of the court is another stone bowl, perhaps for burning
aromatic herbs. Far finer is the bowl in the left apse, a magnificent
contemporary copy in stone of the pottery offering bowls. Its function
is even more conjectural: for the stewing of missionaries has been
suggested. The end of this apse has a structure which could be regarded
as either a roofed niche or an outsized altar. The remaining wall has a

Plate 7. The Central Temple at Tarxien, the central passage and oculus sillstone

very fine trilithon opening, leading into a chamber within the thickness of the wall, with more niches, altars or cupboards.

The corresponding doorway in the right-hand apse has lost its capstone. Beside it is the stump of a massive upright, possibly once as high as that of Ħaġar Qim, which stands in the same relative position as this one to the South Temple. The block cut to fit around its foot supports the similarity. The chamber within this doorway is particularly interesting for the three innermost wall slabs (Plate 8). The first has a low square

Plate 8. Tarxien, the bull-sow-and-piglets and bull reliefs

opening cut through it at ground level, and the relief carving of a bull above it. The second and larger block, nearly 5 metres long in all, has two reliefs, another bull above and a sow with piglets below. The third has a square opening in one bottom corner, giving on to a small space behind the main apse wall.

The reliefs first. The symbolism is almost inescapable, as has been noted already, p. 25, given the association of the very male bull and the patently female sow. But what the carvings should be doing in this inaccessible chamber is another matter. Will the sow help explain the square openings? They look suspiciously like creep feeds. If this room were a pigsty, food could be put in the spaces beyond the openings, where the piglets could reach it but not the sow. But why a pigsty in a temple? And might not the association with the sow relief be entirely coincidental? The bulls have no connection with this interpretation. Once again, one is up against the limitations of guesswork when it comes to interpreting ideas.

Back in the eastern apse, there is an original doorway in its end which leads to the outside. We shall be using it shortly. Inside the door, one of the paving slabs has been lifted to show that they are not mere flags but great blocks as big as any in the temples. If you look back under the even larger threshold slab, you will see still in position one of the stone rollers on which it was manœuvred into place.

The inner apses of this temple are completely separated off by the decorated sill-stone which dominates the court. The double spiral certainly suggests an oculus motif, 'keeping an eye on things'. The slight wear on the original, compared with the much more extensive wear on the modern copy, implies that it was a real barrier and not, as now, just a hazard to be scrambled over. On the other hand, we do not know how solid or immovable the screens were which were held in the same relative position by the rebates, V-perforations and bar-holes in the other doorways. It is possible that access to this innermost, and presumably most sacred, part of the site was by the stairway outside the eastern door, below.

Two of the most finely carved slabs serve as screens to the next apses on either side, with similar but not identical designs based on four spirals. They are best examined in the originals, in the custodian's house. The skilled jointing of the wall orthostats in these apses is worthy of note.

The next passageway is another impressive one. It is floored by an enormous threshold slab, the final surface finishing of which was done after the doorway was erected, as is shown by the little step surviving below the uprights. The central niche beyond this has a slightly wedge-shaped central supporting block. Behind the screen to the left-hand apse is a charming little built-in cupboard, all in stone. The problems raised by the sloping horizontal course of stones above the orthostats in this apse have already been discussed, p. 29.

The right-hand apse has more to tell us. The straight wall at its centre, with a quite different form of tooling, is of Roman date, part of a cellar which destroyed the whole of this apse. Few ancient sites were so completely abandoned as to show no further trace of human activity. Though this wall can only be regarded as an untidiness in the prehistoric site, it too is part of human history and must be respected as such. The rubble apse wall is conjectural modern reconstruction.

Returning to the eastern entrance, we must note two further details. Roman activity is apparent again just outside the door and round to the right. Here is a cistern of Roman date, with associated stone drains. On the other side of the door, squeezed in between the Central and East Temples, is a narrow staircase, the highest surviving steps cut from a single block. It now gives access to the top of the walls, but originally could have served rooms at this upper level, allowed maintenance of the roof, or possibly even have been the main approach, via a wooden stair inside, to the inner 'private' apses of the Central Temple.

The *East Temple* is something of an anticlimax, but should still not be missed. It belongs to the same early Tarxien phase as the South Temple. Its façade is badly damaged and the left-hand apses appear to have been considerably remodelled when the Central Temple was added. Being founded directly on rock, their date cannot be checked from material beneath their floors. The surviving wall of the entrance passage shows a remarkable number of screen supports of various sorts. The right-hand apses have three noteworthy features.

Firstly, the precision cutting of the orthostats is extraordinary. The joints between them are extremely close, considering that they are not straight edges. Were the masons able to carry a slightly sinuous line in their minds accurately from one block to the next, or was it all done by trial and error, the second block being manhandled into position, away for trimming, back, away, and back until the match was considered satisfactory?

Secondly, there is further evidence on the methods of handling the blocks. After they had been brought to the site, perhaps on the stone rollers, and erected, final adjustments were made with big wooden levers. In most of the blocks, a semicircular notch will be noticed at the centre of the long side, designed to take the tip of the lever. The apparent case where a block has been levered up on to a shelf of bedrock is surely illusory. The block was positioned first, and the floor dressed to a level surface afterwards.

Thirdly, between two of the orthostats in the second apse, and pierced right through one in the first, holes communicate with further small intra-mural chambers. These can be approached only from the outside. There are better examples of the same type at Mnajdra, where the function of these so-called Oracle holes will be discussed, p. 102.

Outside the door of the East Temple to the left, though the circular structure is an oven of much later date, the rectangular courtyard beyond is original. An entrance survives at the south-east corner, but the rest of the front wall has gone. Destruction has progressed much further at this end of the site. In the west wall is a porthole slab leading to the chamber behind the rear oracle hole.

Eastwards yet again are the scanty remains of yet a fourth temple. This is the smallest, measuring only 12 metres internally, and the oldest, belonging back in the Ġgantija phase before 2500 B.C. It is typologically early too, since there is a prominent central apse. This puts it into the 5-apse class, although its two eastern apses have vanished. Instead, beneath what was the inner right apse, there is an irregular cavity in the ground. Later enlargement, erosion and other disturbance make interpretation difficult and certainty impossible. We may here have the remains of a rock-cut tomb associated with the temple, an association such as we have already noted at the Hypogeum, though on a vastly more modest scale.

This is the extent of the present remains, but there is ample evidence that originally they spread much more widely. To the south, some fragments have come to light from time to time in the adjacent modern cemetery. Eastwards, one or two large blocks are visible in the lane running behind the site. Immediately to the north, contemporary deposits came to light in 1963. Old and unilluminating records refer to further material on the hill top of Tal Borġ, another 300 metres or so to the north. The Tarxien Temples are only a fragment of what once stood in this area. However, it would be ungracious to complain too bitterly of what has been lost here, when what survives is so fine.

2 · EASTERN MALTA

Whereas the harbour area has lost most of its ancient remains through over-building, eastern and central Malta has suffered equally from agriculture. Wherever the natural surface is the softer globigerina limestone, it can by unremitting toil be turned into arable fields. Wherever it can be, it has been, and wherever ancient sites have hampered the task, they have been destroyed. However, the region still has two major groups of sites and a number of smaller surviving fragments.

The gateway to the eastern end of Malta is the Hompesch Arch at the entrance to Żabbar, surely the saddest triumphal arch anywhere, set up by the last Grand Master of the Order shortly before his ignominious surrender of the island. The ridge running to the north-east of Żabbar has two groups of megaliths, around which prehistoric sherds have been picked up. One lies on the right-hand side of the road a kilometre south-east of the Naval Cemetery, the other immediately to the west of Fort Leonardo, San Anard. Neither yields an interpretable plan, so has little to tempt the short-term visitor.

The next ridge, south of the Żabbar–Marsaskala road, has more of interest. A kilometre short of Marsaskala, a lane climbs south to Bidni. On the left of it is an interesting calvary. 300 metres west of the chapel Tad-Dawl is a feature known as Ic-Ċirku, the Circle. It is not, as was for long thought, a Roman amphitheatre, appropriate though its form is, but a karstic depression like those of the Maqluba and Qawra. On bare rock 100 metres south-east of the chapel is the Bidni dolmen, small but characteristic. Remains of another are built into a field wall to the south-west, and there may once have been a small cemetery here.

Marsaskala is a pleasant little fishing village, with a series of artificial fishponds. After a raid by corsairs in 1614, its safety was ensured by the building of St Thomas's Tower at the mouth of the inlet. 200 metres south-west of this is a site of great interest, recommended only for the intrepid. A shaft in a field gives on to not the usual bell-shaped field cistern (cf. Tal Mejtin, p. 88) but the passage of a small family catacomb, now serving the same purpose. The original entrance is blocked.

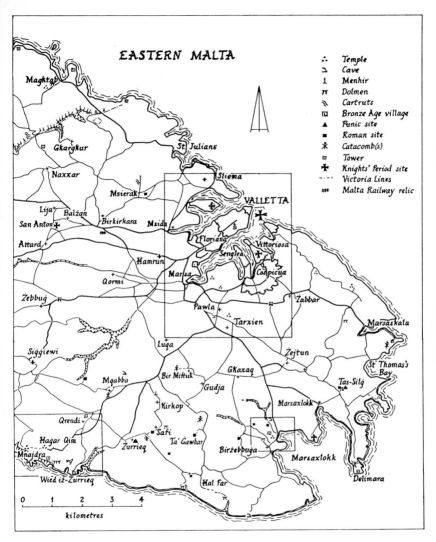

Fig. 13. East Malta, the archaeological sites

For those prepared to brave the descent (a torch is essential) and the 50 cms. or so of cold water at the bottom, varying with season, a panel beside one of the side chambers bears the only explicitly Christian inscription in any of the Maltese catacombs. It reads: In nomine domini Jesu Christi surge et ambula—Domine salvum me fac.

Żejtun was one of the original Maltese parishes, and fortunately has kept its early church, San Girgor or St Gregory. This is on the eastern edge of the village, peaceful, unassuming, and illustrative of what parish churches were like before Malta had felt the impact of baroque in the 17th century. At the feast of Saint Gregory on the first Wednesday after Easter, it is the object of pilgrimage for many Maltese. After attending mass here, they repair for more secular celebration to the seaside at Marsaxlokk.

A megalithic site was excavated at Ħal Ġinwi, 1·5 kilometres south-east of Żejtun, by Dr Laferla in 1917. Its stonework can still be identi-fied in field walls 100 metres south of the chapel of San Nicola. It had an irregular plan, but the finds showed clearly that it had been built by the temple people.

The hill of Tas-Silġ, to be described in the next section, overlooks the northern arm of Marsaxlokk (Marsascirocco) Bay and the very pic-turesque fishing village of *Marsaxlokk* itself. This was where the Turkish army came ashore in 1565, and the skeletons which turn up from time to time to the south of the village may have been some of their many casualties. The Torre Cavallerizza and, even more obviously, Fort St Lucian were built to dominate the bay and prevent any repeat of the events of that summer.

The cliffs, bays and headlands between Marsaxlokk Bay and St Thomas's Bay provide some unexpected scenery, some good bathing and a temple site which, if much ruined, has a most impressive situation. This is on top of a 30 metre cliff on the east side of the *Xrobb il-Għaġin* promontory. It was dug in 1914 to reveal the remains of a typical four-apse temple. Its pleasant-sounding name means literally 'spaghetti water', referring to the pasty appearance of the sea below when in rough weather it erodes the soft pale rock of the cliffs.

We must return to the hilltop of *Tas-Silġ*. The name comes from the chapel on its southern slope, dedicated to Our Lady of the Snows. Malta, having no experience of natural snow, frost or ice, has to use the word for hail, silġ, to cover all. Classical ruins have been known here since the time of Jacques Houel in the late 18th century, when con-siderably more was visible than a few years ago. A series of campaigns of excavation by the Italian Missione Archeologica since 1963, and still continuing, is revealing in detail the history of the site. An enclosure wall has been added, the key to which is kept at the farm beyond the San Nicola chapel.

There are four principal periods of occupation. In the first a temple was built in the Tarxien phase on the crest of the ridge, north of the road and just inside the eastern boundary wall. Drastic later alterations make the plan rather difficult to elucidate, but it seems best to interpret it as a close parallel to the central unit at Ħaġar Qim. There are four apses and apparently a back door in place of the central niche. The main question is, which is back and which front? The eastern door as the main entrance would be in agreement with the usual orientation of the temples as a whole. On the other hand there are clear traces of a concave façade on either side of the western door, and the carved figure found in the south-west apse might suggest that this was the first apse on the right, by analogy with Tarxien.

Following the collapse of the temples, Bronze Age material was scattered freely over the hill, mainly in the area south of the road. Later disturbance of these levels has destroyed for all time the evidence on whether this represents continuity of sanctity of the temple, or coincidental re-use of an obvious site, as at Borġ in-Nadur, Skorba or Tarxien.

The site's most important period begins, according to the excavators, about the end of the 6th century B.C. and continues to the 1st A.D., with most of the extant structures belonging to the latter part of this span. The final report should make the details clear. During this time it was again a religious site, a temple dedicated to Astarte/Hera. Dedications to both goddesses, or to the one goddess under both her Phoenician and Greek names, have been found in some numbers. It is best described as Punic throughout, although the East Mediterranean influence appears to be much stronger than the North African, and although the island was in Roman possession from 218 B.C. on. It is suggested that this, indeed, was the Temple of Juno which Verres despoiled in 73–71 B.C.

Structurally the prehistoric ruin was refurbished as the sanctuary of the temple, now with its entrance firmly to the west. A colonnaded court or hall was added, and some ancillary buildings. A great enclosure, or temenos, wall was built around it, of which a 28 metre stretch can be seen south of the modern road.

There follows a curious and unexplained hiatus until the 4th century A.D., when the site was once again adapted to a new religion, Christianity. It is interpreted at this period as a monastery. The old prehistoric temple became a baptistery, with a central font added, the hall the main church, and many additional buildings appeared around. Decay followed in the 6th century. A few lengths of wall could be dated to the Arab period by their associated pottery, but this occupation, lying so near the field surface, had been too mutilated to tell us much.

Outside the enclosure wall to the north-west, the exceptionally large cistern of Bir Rica was presumably cut to serve the temple site.

All in all, a fascinating site. Until a definitive report appears, visitors will enjoy trying to puzzle out the details of the remains for themselves.

The modern village of Birżebbuġa is the largest on Marsaxlokk Bay, and is connected by main road with Valletta. As the road drops towards the head of St George's Bay, the *Għar Dalam* Museum and car park lie on the right (Fig. 14).

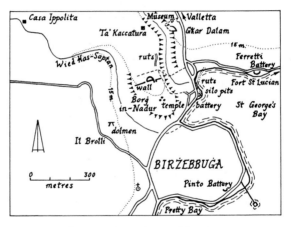

Fig. 14. Birżebbuġa and its sites

The museum houses a small but impressive fraction of the semi-fossilized bones of Malta's Pleistocene fauna. They are thought to date to the Great Interglacial, now placed about 250,000 years ago. The animal most commonly represented is the hippopotamus, *H. pentlandi*, a stunted form it is true but clear proof of a very different landscape from that of the islands today. Also present were three dwarf species of elephant, *Elephas mnaidrensis*, *E. melitensis* and *E. falconeri*. The last and smallest reached only the size of a St Bernard dog. By contrast there was a swan of giant size. Their presence confirms a land connection at this date with Sicily, and isolation from the south. With deteriorating climate, the hippopotamus and elephants were driven out of Europe except here and in other Mediterranean islands, where they could retreat no further. Their decreasing size suggests adverse conditions for growth, adversity in due course leading to extinction.

A higher level in the cave yielded great numbers of red deer bones, and was probably laid down in the cool wet period of the closing stages of the last ice age, some 10,000 years ago. No trace of human occupation has been found in either of these levels.

Later still, the cave was occupied irregularly from the time of the first human settlement down to the date of the excavations, from 1911 on. The resulting accumulation of deposit was thin and much disturbed, but produced some interesting material of the early Neolithic, for which it was chosen as the type site. The Borġ in-Nadur phase was well represented too. Two human teeth gave rise to much controversy. They were of the taurodont form, with a single large hollow root, found commonly in Neanderthal Man. But this form is known, if rarely, in modern man too—one was extracted from the jaw of a living Maltese only a few years ago—and so does not prove the presence of Neanderthalers here. Careful chemical analysis at the British Museum (Natural History) in 1959 confirmed that these teeth were contemporary with the bones of domestic animals, more recent than the deer bones, and much more recent than the fossil fauna. It was similar analysis which suggested that the hippopotamus tooth implicated in the Piltdown forgery probably came from this same site.

The mounted skeletons in the centre cases of the museum are of modern animals, displayed for comparative purposes.

The custodian conducts visitors down steps into the Wied Dalam, in the slope of which opens the cave itself (Plate 9). This was dissolved from the limestone by percolating ground water to leave an enormous cavity 7·30 metres across and 5·50 high. It runs straight back into the hill, the first 70 metres being artificially illuminated. It is possible to penetrate further with torches, but the main passage divides into much smaller and muddier ones, the longest being blocked by inwashed clay some 50 metres beyond.

A pillar of the original deposits has been left in the centre of the cave to demonstrate their succession. Several areas of the most interesting, the bone breccia, have been left exposed. Many explanations for this accumulation of dismembered bones (though at least one hippopotamus

6

Plate 9. Għar Dalam, interior. The block and pillar on the
right show the level and nature of the original deposits

leg can be recognized still articulated) have been offered, but none is
universally accepted.

A rough path descends from the mouth of the cave to cross the valley
floor and climb the slope opposite to the extensive ruins of a Roman
country house, the site known as *Ta' Kaċċatura*. The walls stand to no
great height and the overall plan is hard to determine. The great underground water cistern above still makes the visit worth while. It is walled
to prevent accidents; the custodian at the Għar Dalam Museum should
be asked for the key. The cistern is cut some 5·50 metres into the rock,
a flight of steps having been left for access. It was once completely
roofed with stone slabs at ground level, supported on great pillars
built of squared stone blocks, but some of the roof slabs have since fallen.

The Birżebbuġa road continues from the Museum down to meet St
George's Bay, an inlet of Marsaxlokk. Overlooking this from the south
is the limestone ridge of *Borġ in-Nadur*, left by the erosion of the two
valleys, Wied Dalam and Wied Ħas-Saptan. The ridge can be reached
either by a scramble along its crest from Ta' Kaċċatura, or by a path

following the oil pipelines behind the Shell depot, or by a lane from the end of Nadur Street, right and right again from the main road.

The antiquities belong to two periods, both prehistoric. Near the tip of the promontory is a group of ruins within a massive original enclosure wall, and there is an outlying group of megaliths to the south. They date to the last phase of the temple period, shortly before 2000 B.C. Though its walls are only half a metre high, a four-apse temple plan can be easily distinguished at the centre. But the shallowness of the deposits made the site's history difficult for the excavators, Dr Margaret Murray and her party in 1922–7, to disentangle. The temple period material was outweighed by fragments of the Bronze Age phase since named after this site, and the two could not be separated stratigraphically. For example, a sherd of Mycenaean IIIB pottery, dated to *c.* 1240 B.C., has been recognized among the finds, but only external evidence showed to which occupation (the later) it belonged.

It seems, indeed, as if the ruins of the temple, desecrated by the

Plate 10. Borġ in-Nadur, the Bronze Age defensive wall with Fort St Lucian, Delimara Point and the waters of Marsaxlokk behind

Bronze Age invaders, were adapted as dwellings, hovels rather, by the newcomers. In fields to the north-west, proper hut foundations built for the purpose were discovered in 1881 and again in 1959. The trenches were refilled after the excavations. Bronze Age sherds scattered over the whole promontory suggest that it supported a sizable village at this time, the later 2nd millennium B.C.

The most noteworthy relic is the defensive wall which protects the only part of the village where an attack could be mounted over level ground, the neck of the promontory (Plate 10). At the centre of the wall, a massive D-shaped redoubt projected, and it is here that the wall, standing to some 4·50 metres high, is at its most impressive. It was exposed by A. A. Caruana in 1881, the great bank in front of it being the spoil he pulled back. The smaller stonework in this wall, and its internal face, are modern restoration. The present entrance to the south of the bastion is also recent, at least in its present form. To the north of the bastion, a stretch of the old wall can be recognized turning in to protect what must have been the original gateway. It is worth mention that on the bare rock to the north-west, beyond the path, a pair of cart-ruts may be made out heading for this point.

Returning to the road, visitors should glance over the further wall at the sea edge. Towards the head of the bay is the famous pair of cart-ruts which 'run out to sea'. They cannot be followed on the sea bed, having been scoured away by the wave-rolled pebbles, but could be picked up again until a few years ago re-emerging beyond the head of the bay some 50 metres off. To the right, where the coast bends back towards the village below a Knights' redoubt, a group of bell-shaped openings in the rock up to a metre across can be clearly seen. Some are truncated by quarrying and all are more or less filled with sea water. They cannot be dated directly. By analogy with Baħrija and Nuffara, we may guess them to be silo pits associated with the Bronze Age village or rather, as they lie well outside the defences, perhaps with a small port below.

Neither the ruts nor silo pits, of course, make sense in their present position, but to explain them we need suggest no more than a 1·50 metre rise in sea level over the last 3,000 years. Much greater variations than this have been documented on the western coast of Italy. The rise may well have been greater, but in any case these ruts are not heading off for Africa, as has been suggested.

At Il Brolli, 400 metres north-west of the parish church of Birżebbuġa, a dolmen lies in fields to the right of a country lane. Just south of the junction of this lane with another from Gudja, a kilometre beyond, a Roman cistern can be seen in the verge.

The main road continues through Birżebbuġa, past a series of Knights' period defences to *Kalafrana*. This used to be a key staging point for sea-planes on the imperial route to India. A right turn leads up to Hal Far, p. 89.

3 · THE CENTRAL PLAIN

The heart of Malta, from Mosta and Għargħur to the edge of Luqa Airport, is remarkably devoid of ancient remains. It is difficult to tell how far, as we have suggested for East Malta, this can be blamed on the intensive agriculture, or in the area between Lija and Marsamxett Harbour on the blanketing by modern settlement. Occupation there certainly was, as is shown by a few scattered finds. At L'Imsieraħ, west of Sliema, are the scanty remains of the round tower of Ta' Ċieda. At Mensija close by are cart-ruts, and a group of Early Bronze Age pots, perhaps the remains of a smaller Tarxien Cemetery, was recently discovered. Bronze Age tombs were found beside what later became Ta' Qali aerodrome in 1912. The much older tombs discovered in 1947 at Ta' Trapna, a mile west of Żebbuġ, were important enough to give the name of Żebbuġ to one of the phases of pottery development. But few of these sites have left anything to see on the ground, and none is worth much of a detour.

Of more recent date are the great Mosta Dome (completed 1860), the graffiti of the 18th century galleys on the Qlejgħa chapel (1·5 kilometres west of Mosta where the Mġarr road crosses the gorge), and the San Anton Palace (1620's) and its delightful gardens between Balżan, Lija and Attard. For the industrial archaeologist there are the traces of the Malta Railway, which from 1883 to 1931 connected Valletta with Rabat. The former station at Birkirkara is especially noteworthy. And for the botanist, good hunting is to be had in the rocky gorges of the Wied tal-Isperanza north of Mosta, the Wied Inċita south of Attard and the Wied il-Kbir and its branches south of Qormi.

A further site in this area deserves mention if only as a curiosity. In the Wied Qirda a short distance upstream from its confluence with the Wied il-Kbir an artificial cave opens high in the southern cliff. One suspects the influence of Achaemenid Persia, particularly the tomb of Darius at Naqsh-i Rustam. It is indeed said to be a tomb, of an eccentric English lady in the last century. This might be an appropriate moment to tell of another Englishwoman who has entered Maltese tradition—

the misguided lady, quite mythical incidentally, who introduced the attractive little yellow oxalis, *O. capensis* or Bermuda sorrel, to her flower garden in Malta. Thence it spread rapidly, with the Maltese name of 'ħaxixa ingliża', the Englishwoman's weed, to become the most pernicious plant pest in the islands. But there is no denying that it adds a great deal to the scenery.

Immediately south of the Wied il-Kbir, sites of greater archaeological interest begin again. Between the head of the Wied ta' Kandja and the lane bordering the south-west corner of the airport enclosure, a kilometre west of Mqabba, is the *Torri ta' Wilġa*. Excavation by Ashby in 1908 was inconclusive, giving a date 'not earlier than Punic', so it is the comparative evidence of Ta' Ġawhar (p. 89) which allows us to place this great circular tower in the Roman period, about the 3rd century A.D.

Across the lane towards *Mqabba* an early Christian catacomb was found when the main airport runway was extended in 1960 (Plate 11). It could not be preserved—there were obvious difficulties to diverting the runway round it. Visitors will be amused to learn that they have been within a few feet of a site even before they step out of their plane. A much earlier casualty of the airfield was a megalithic site of the temple

Plate 11. A field catacomb near Mqabba, now under Luqa Airport runway. The entrance and arcosolium tombs

period at Debdieba, a kilometre north of Mqabba. No clear plan emerged in the excavation of 1908, so its loss is probably not very serious.

A little to the east again, a small cave containing temple period pottery was discovered in quarrying at Bur Mgħeż in 1910. This area is one of the main ones for extracting the 'franca' building stone, and there is no telling what sites may not have been quarried away in the process.

In the southern edge of the village of Mqabba are two small late Roman catacombs at Tal Mintna (key again in the National Museum). They have finely carved canopied and arcosolium tombs (see p. 116). The small field chapel of the Annunciation at Ħal Millieri a kilometre south-east of the village has been recently cleared to reveal fragments of wall paintings dating to the 15th century A.D.

South-east of *Luqa* towards Gudja are three sites of note. In the fields opposite the Luqa village cemetery a series of water cisterns have come to light. They are of the bell-shaped form, up to 3·40 metres in diameter at the base and 4 metres deep. Two of them at least yielded Bronze Age pottery, together with unexpected evidence on Malta's prehistoric vegetation, preserved in the waterlogged clay of their fill, the nastiest deposit I have ever had the misfortune to dig through. Grains of plant pollen were extracted and identified to show that by the Bronze Age Malta's vegetation was already much as it is today—grass and low herbs, Mediterranean scrub, and a little, but very little, pollen of the pine and (probably cultivated) olive. Any tree cover the island may once have had must have been cleared by the end of the temple period.

Three hundred metres further towards Gudja, the road bends sharply past the old church of Santa Marija ta' *Bir Miftuħ*. This, like San Girgor at Żejtun, was the church of one of the great medieval parishes, though now completely isolated. The present structure goes back to 1436, with a few later alterations.

A lane runs west from the bend in the road north of the chapel, and passes after 400 metres a small square building with a green iron door. This opens to a key held in the National Museum to reveal one of the most charming of Malta's field catacombs, that known as *Ħal Resqun*. A flight of steps in the rock leads to a small chamber with an agape table (see p. 114). The modern masonry partly obscuring it hides the pipe-line which disclosed the site in 1912. Two burial chambers of the two-berth type open on either side. One is modestly decorated, the other, facing the stairs, has two fascinating engraved scenes. On the wall above it are two outline birds, probably pelicans, iconographically if not ornithologically. Immediately above the entrance are a number of animal and human figures packed into a very small space, horizontally, vertically or even inverted. The meaning of this scene is quite obscure. The Garden of Eden has been suggested, but who might the third human figure be?

A sprinkle of sites continues right to the southern cliffs. Half way between Luqa and Hal Far airfields, the road connecting them loops round the gentle ridge of Tal Liebru. On the top of this is another field catacomb, containing engraved crosses. However, the landowner at the time of writing discourages visitors. Maltese dogs bark worse than they bite, and this was one of only two occasions, despite a great deal of trespassing on my part, on which I got bitten.

Five hundred metres farther on, a lane bears back to the right, due west to Safi. A hundred metres along this, a narrow track to the south leads to a ruined farmhouse beside the Roman tower of *Ta' Gawhar*. Excavation in 1960 showed this to be a defensive work of the 3rd century A.D., probably to be associated with the incursion of the Heruli from the Black Sea into the Mediterranean in 269. It may be one of a planned series, since there are the scanty remains of two more such towers 1·2 kilometres to the south-west and 1·3 kilometres to the south of this one. The Torri ta' Wilġa was noticed on p. 87, west of Mqabba, and there are others, more ruinous, at L'Imsieraħ, west of Sliema, and at Għajn Klieb and Tas-Santi, commanding one of the roads over the Bengemma Hills. Ta' Gawhar is the best preserved. Its outer wall, 2·40 metres thick, still stands at one point to a height of over 5 metres (Plate 12). One of its four internal rooms was cleared, showing it to have been turned into a farmhouse or the like after the scare had passed. But it was destroyed by fire soon after, leaving such things as an iron axe, two bronze buckets, a gold ear-ring, and a carbonized bread roll beneath its ashes. Archaeologists rightly stress the information given by their finds rather than their market value, but it is difficult to remain unmoved when gold falls to one's own trowel. However, I would rate the bread roll an equal treasure. The finds are now all in the Roman Villa Museum at Rabat, together with a fine carved architectural block.

Beside the tower to the east was cut a water cistern similar to, though much smaller than, that at Ta' Kaċċatura (p. 82). Two pillars were sufficient to support its slab roof. On this side of the tower, excavation showed that there had been Bronze Age occupation here before the tower itself was built.

Like Luqa, *Hal Far* airfield took its toll of antiquities. A megalithic

Plate 12. The Roman round tower at Ta' Ġawhar

site was destroyed, and an isolated menhir was moved to a less inconvenient position at the main entrance of the Naval Air Station. One of Malta's few dolmens fortunately lay beyond the line of the runways and so could be spared. It stands on the western lip of the *Wied Żnuber* near its head, between the centre of the airfield and the sea (Plate 13). It is a burial chamber thought to belong to the Early Bronze Age, a little after 2000 B.C., and consists of a flat slab of rock some 1·20 metres across, supported horizontally above the ground on smaller rocks.

Għar Hassan, a cave opening in the lip of the sea cliffs a kilometre to the south-east (access is signposted from the Ħal Far–Kalafrana road) is rich in legend but has yielded no material remains. It is reputed to have been the home for some time of Hassan, the last Saracen on the island after its reconquest by the Normans.

If one turns to the north-west, the Ħal Far–Żurrieq road passes after 400 metres the *Tal Bakkari* crossroads, where the foundations of a medieval chapel (Santa Marija) were uncovered in 1922, and where traces of a second round tower can be made out in field walls immediately to the south. A lane to the left just beyond leads down to the

Plate 13. The Wied Żnuber dolmen

Wied Moqbol or Maqbul. Circular cairns on its western lip were dated in 1953 to the Tarxien Cemetery phase. Another kilometre towards Żurrieq brings one level with the low hill to the right bearing the third round tower in this district, also in poor shape and not easy to find among the numerous field walls.

A more prominent landmark is provided by Malta's last remaining windmill—Gozo still has two. Windmill towers will frequently be noticed, but Safi's retains its sails, a memorial to the not-so-distant days when all Malta's corn was ground by wind power. The road from here into *Safi* village passes on its right a length of Roman walling, though too little survives to make interpretation possible. On the east side of the village (the lanes are too confusing for written instructions to be of much help) is another dolmen like that of Wied Żnuber.

Beside the road just north of *Kirkop* is Malta's finest menhir, a stone pillar of square section some 3 metres high. Its date and function are alike unknown—the cross carved from its top is probably a much later addition.

Żurrieq, a populous village, has only one antiquity of note, but a very

extraordinary one. It is a square tower, measuring 3 metres a side and
5·60 metres high, standing in the garden of the parish priest. An appoint-
ment to visit it should be arranged beforehand. A cavetto cornice
moulding around its top has a very Egyptian appearance, so a date in the
Phoenician period is likely, if unproved. Exploratory excavation inside
and around it has given no clear result, the ground has been too much
disturbed. If the date is correct, this tower is our only upstanding
monument from these six centuries of Malta's past. It may perhaps have
been a monumental tomb.

One and a half kilometres west of Żurrieq is *Qrendi* (Fig. 15). A
kilometre beyond, on the south side of the road to Siġġiewi, stands

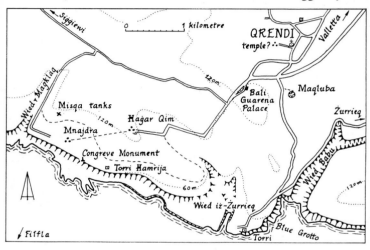

Fig. 15. Qrendi and its sites

another fine dolmen, the *Misrah ta' Sinjura*. The impression it gives is
somewhat marred by the deep quarries cut round it, and the square
field hut perched incongruously on its capstone, but it must originally
have been one of Malta's best.

In Qrendi itself, the tower of a fortified farm in the northern edge of
the village, is worth a glance in passing. It is octagonal with projecting
machicolations, more graphically called 'drop-boxes', at its top. It is
late medieval in date. Along the lane running west from the church, a
few large stones hint at another much ruined building of the temple
period.

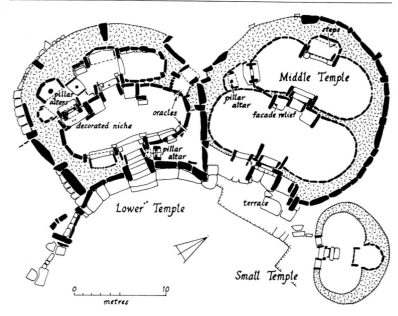

Fig. 17. The Mnajdra Temples

Valletta Museum, this is the only one carved on part of a temple structure. Its purpose is quite unknown. Note on this same slab how the final dressing of the stone was carried out after the altar was placed against it.

Through this passage, the inner apses repeat the usual pattern. The central niche is roofed at head height, like one at Tarxien. Toe holds on its rear wall give access to an upper level in the thickness of the wall, but the proof that they were cut in the temple period is lacking. The stairway to the upper level at Tarxien, however, supports the possibility. In the left-hand corner of the inner apses, a fine porthole slab within a trilithon opens on to a tiny chamber in the wall thickness which contains a good example of a pillar-supported altar.

The third temple, built early in the Tarxien phase and so the second in date, opens on to the court at a lower level. Most visitors will support the view that it is the finest surviving temple, though the southern of the two at the Ġgantija and the central one at Tarxien run it close. Its

Plate 17. The lower temple at Mnajdra: the forecourt and façade (*above*) and the decorated niche and pillar altars (*below*)

markedly concave façade is of the standard pattern, with bench, orthostats and trilithon entrance (Plate 17). Note the small conical stone
standing upright on the left of the door, perhaps another betyl. Inside
the rude outer wall, the masonry is sophisticated in planning and
workmanship, made possible by the use of the softer limestone here.
All this stone has had to be transported from the brow of the hill above,
where it outcrops.

Plate 18. Mnajdra, the right-hand apse of the lower temple, with doorway and
oracle holes

The centre of interest in the first apse is in the left inner corner. Here there is a magnificent porthole slab framed in a trilithon, the whole decorated all over by close-spaced pitting (Plate 17). Examination will show that this was produced with some sort of drill and further, from the angle of drilling in the less accessible corners, was carried out after the structure was erected. V-perforations presumably held a door or screen to bar the inner chamber. Beneath this doorway is a great threshold slab, carefully cut to fit around the orthostats. And on either side are free-standing pitted slabs widening upwards like that in the outer wall shrine at Ħaġar Qim.

The chamber through this doorway is in effect the inner left apse of the temple, separated from its partner by a double altar with pillar supports. A similar pillared altar lies opposite the doorway and a third, pitted but without a pillar, to the left of it. Here too one would badly like to know what ceremonies took place on and around these altars. The rest of the inner apses has little of note. The apparent crudity of the masonry in the right apse was almost certainly originally masked by plaster.

The first apse on the right, however, will detain us a bit longer (Plate 18). The oversailing walls rise over 4 metres from floor level, and here as much as anywhere one can feel oneself to be inside a building rather than wandering over, or at best through its ruins. Note that the upper courses of blocks have an inward tilt, the significance of which was discussed on p. 29. In the eastern wall is an attractive little doorway, with a stepped approach and another porthole slab. It leads to a small chamber within the wall thickness. To the right is one of the most sophisticated of the altar niches, porthole slab within trilithon, leading to an altar slab supported on an elaborate pillar. Here it is especially noticeable that all 'straight' lines are, in fact, slightly bowed out, as if the blocks were not of stone but of a soft cheese which had settled a little under its own weight. This creates an impression of great stability. This can hardly be said of the opposite wall, the outer temple wall until the middle temple was erected against it. It is not really so dangerous as it looks and, having lasted nearly $4\frac{1}{2}$ thousand years, will, one hopes, hold up a little while longer.

This chamber communicates with the main apse also by a perforation through the slab next to the doorway. In actual fact, it is more accurately a square notch in the side of the stone, patched with a smaller block, perhaps after an accident in the cutting. An even better example can be seen through the third block to the left, this one opening from an even smaller intra-mural chamber, approached from outside the temple altogether. Much speculation has arisen from these, and the similar examples at Tarxien and Ħaġar Qim. They are commonly known as 'oracle holes', it being supposed that a worshipper could receive through them instructions or information from the gods through the medium of a priest secreted in the chamber behind. The layout can be held to support the worshipper/priest relationship, though we ought perhaps to use 'priest' in a very general sense. But the nature of what passed between them is not only pure guesswork: it must always remain so. Offerings or confessions in one direction, advice, orders, talismans, healing, in the other, by no means exhaust all the possibilities. In this temple, more perhaps than in any other, we come tantalizingly close to the beliefs and rituals of its builders, whilst remaining aware that further progress in understanding is probably impossible.

Returning to the main courtyard, we find that the third temple's façade is continued as a free-standing screen, very much as at the Ġgantija. At its end is a panelled block, D-shaped in plan with a fitted paving slab before it. A frieze of bulls has been claimed, in certain lights, on its face. Perhaps I have never seen it in the right light. It would be easy to reconstruct in the mind's eye a carved goddess figure too, standing on this plinth and overlooking the forecourt, but this is pure speculation.

On the very crest of the hill, 200 metres inland from the temples, are the *Misqa Tanks*. These are a group of enormous water cisterns cut in the rock. Though not particularly close in form to the undoubted temple period cistern in the Hypogeum (p. 59), they are not unlike the example at Tarxien and do not fall into any other recognized category, Bronze Age, Roman, medieval or modern. They may well, then, have been cut to supply the needs of the temple. Repeated clearings seem to have removed any original deposit which might have dated them. Despite the promontory in which they are cut, they fill rapidly with surface run-off during the autumn rains, and are still used to irrigate the surrounding fields.

4 · WEST MALTA

'Highland' Malta consists of a triangular block of country between Mdina and the sea cliffs (Fig. 18). The escarpment of the upper coralline limestone delimits it on all sides, providing startling constrasts between the open plateau above, often with much bare rock exposed, and the secluded, sheltered valleys below, well watered by the springs that break out on the clay at the foot of the cliffs. Apart from the escarpment itself, the relief is not marked. The highest point on the island lies close to Dingli, at 252 metres above mean sea level, but there is no obvious peak.

MDINA

The old capital of Malta, known variously as Melita, Mdina and Città Notabile, occupies the most attractive of the eastern promontories (Fig. 19). Topography alone is sufficient to mark it out for this role—its scarps, water in the valley to the north, convenient area, and above all its dominating position, overlooking the whole central plain (Plate 19).

The visible remains go back at most to the Arab occupation, but in 1962 heavy Roman masonry, perhaps part of the town walls, was found beneath the rear courtyard of the Vilhena Palace and on the slope at the foot of the fortifications to the east. Further, amongst the debris disturbed by Roman building was pottery of the Middle Bronze Age. A village of this period could already be suspected on a steep-sided promontory like this, the type of position so obviously preferred. It probably had a wall like that of Borġ in-Nadur barring the approach, perhaps on the line of the later defences of Mdina, but if so, no trace has come to light.

The size of the Phoenician town on the site we do not know either. Roman Melita took in Rabat as far south-west as the parish church, as will be seen shortly. The Arabs, after a period of seriously declining population, withdrew to the tip again, and began the fortifications which,

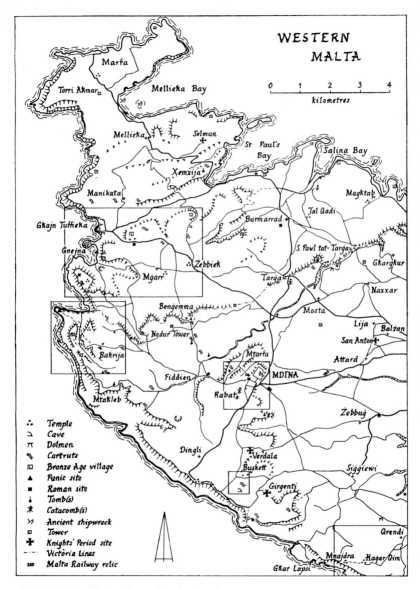

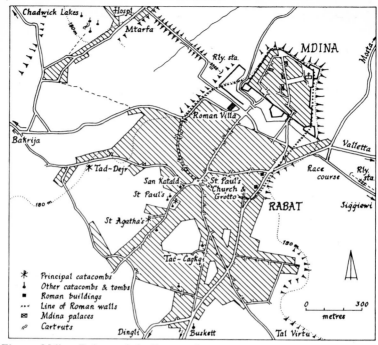

Fig. 19. Mdina, Rabat and the Roman city

Plate 19. Mdina and Rabat from the air. Mtarfa lies to the left and St Paul's Bay, with the islets, and Salina Bay in the distance

Plate 20. The entrance of Mdina Cathedral on a feast day

greatly strengthened in the medieval and Knights' periods, survive to the present day. The jambs of their gateway are visible in the wall face to the right of the present main gate, which was moved westwards by Grand Master de Vilhena in 1724 to make more room for his palace within.

Rabat developed as a suburb of the old city from the 17th century on, when the expanding population spilled over the Mdina walls, an expansion which passed beyond the former line of the Roman walls in the 19th century and is continuing to the south and west today.

Mdina's antiquities, then, are not very old, though still of some interest. The walls in their present form are largely of the 16th/17th century; the cathedral (Plate 20), reputedly on the site of Publius's official residence, was entirely rebuilt after an earthquake in 1697, to plans of Lorenzo Gafà; the Vilhena Palace was erected in 1730 to house the courts of justice. There are several late medieval town houses, notably the so-called Norman House, Palazzo Santa Sofia, the Palazzo Gatto Murena and the Palazzo Re Ferdinando (see plan). At the far end of the town, one can linger long over the panorama from the bastions. Here is the best place on clear winter or spring days to look for Mount

Etna, 210 kilometres away but still an imposing sight, rising unbeliev-
ably high above the northern horizon.

But certainly the most memorable aspect of Mdina is its atmosphere,
the quiet streets and the views out from the bastions. The cathedral
clock gives the minute, hour, day and month, but not the year. Years do
not matter here.

RABAT

In the modern town of Rabat, little is left of its classical predecessor
owing to the overbuilding in later times. Mr Mallia of the National
Museum is currently bringing to light fragments in the Saqqaja
Square area, including a mosaic floor set on a bed of wine amphorae, but
later constructions severely limit the extent and preservation of the
remains. In the ruins known as the *Roman Villa*, however, we have a
fine example of what there once was.

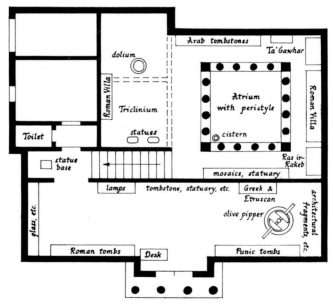

Fig. 20. The Roman Villa and Museum of Roman Antiquities,
Rabat

This building (Fig. 20), over which has been built the *Museum of Roman Antiquities*, overlooks the valley to the north of Mdina–Rabat. Its preservation is the result of its lying in the zone outside the Mdina walls kept open for defensive purposes, now largely occupied by the Howard Gardens. It was discovered and excavated by Caruana in 1881, with further work and restoration in 1921–3, when the museum was added on to it.

One approaches the Museum first. In the portico are a few carved and inscribed blocks of stone from the area. The main gallery has many more along its back wall and at the north-east end, some of high quality. Unfortunately three of the most eye-catching are suspect. The marble Hercules, reputed to have been found at the Phoenician temple at Marsaxlokk (Tas-Silġ?) in the later 18th century, is almost certainly Neapolitan work of only a few years earlier than the date of its 'discovery'. The reliefs of Zenobia and Penthesilea are equally dubious. But there is better to come, such as the tombstone of the lyre-player from Pergamum, dating to about A.D. 150.

The olive pipper, reconstituted in the centre of the hall at its northern end, is a worthy symbol of the Roman prosperity of the island, and came from Marsaxlokk. The olives were crushed between the revolving stone discs and the interior of the bowl, without damaging their pips. The mush would then have been transferred to a press to extract the oil. Other examples have been found in situ at San Pawl Milqgħi and sporadic in Gozo.

The cases along the front wall are devoted to material from some of the great number of tombs around the city (Plate 21). It is a little premature to discuss these in detail as the careful work on ordering and dating them has barely been started. One serious difficulty has been that tombs were frequently reopened for the addition of later burials. This means that one cannot assume that the contents of any one tomb, even if found sealed, are necessarily of one period. However, typological study, coupled with the occasional discovery of datable imports, allows some progress to be made. For example, a group from Ġnien is-Sultan in the last case on the right includes a proto-Corinthian cup. Most of the Phoenician-type pots with it would fit happily in the same 7th-century context. Some, however, would not, and represent a reopening of the tomb, perhaps in the 2nd or 1st century B.C., to add another interment. Certainly it is not difficult to distinguish the general run of Punic pottery, with its thicker wares, purple painted rings, *bilychnis* lamps (saucers with lips infolded to leave two spouts) and the like, from full

Plate 21. A Punic tomb at Tal Horr, Pawla, as found

Roman (thinner bowls and cups, red slip, subsidiary vessels in glass, etc.). The cultural change, however, came very slowly, some 200 years after the Roman occupation in 218 B.C., and was never truly completed. Maltese provincial Roman retained a Punic flavour to the end.

Above the cases are amphorae, the great storage jars for wine and oil, which have also come mostly from tombs. The egg-shaped ones, round-bottomed and neck-less, derive from Phoenician originals and are typically Maltese. Those with pointed bases and long necks and handles were of the standard form throughout the Roman Empire, and can be closely matched as far off as Britain.

The other cases contain more general material, mostly without known provenance, and so grouped by type rather than by site. The Greek and Etruscan pottery in the north-west corner case has a varied history. The fine proto-Corinthian cup of the 7th century B.C. was excavated from a tomb at Mtarfa by Zammit in 1924. The red-figure vases, late Attic, 5th to 4th century B.C., were found at Rabat a hundred years earlier, and are correspondingly less well documented. The Etruscan burial cists, 8th/7th century, are fine, but there is no record of how or when they reached Malta, probably as antiques in very recent times.

The lamps in the south-west corner case show the history of these useful vessels from Phoenician to medieval times. The Imperial Roman ones, with their moulded medallions, are the most interesting. The earlier, usually buff-coloured, ones have purely pagan designs, while on the later red ones the chi-rho monogram and other Christian symbolism is patent. This latter group was mass-produced in enormous numbers in 4th/5th-century Tunisia, after Christianity had become respectable.

The glass-ware on the other side of the doorway is worthy of note too. One must remember, however, that the iridescence which gives it so much of its charm was the result of physical changes after burial. Its original makers and owners would have seen it completely transparent. But there are some fragments of deliberately coloured glass, blues and greens, as well.

Through the doorway, a staircase descends to the Roman ground level. At its head is a large block with a fulsome inscription, the pedestal of a statue to a public benefactor, dating to the reign of Hadrian. It yields some historical information; that the city of Melita held the status of a *municipium* for example. The walls of the staircase bear plans of the Villa and of the Roman Baths at Għajn Tuffieħa (p. 141), and drawings of the mosaics from these two sites.

Plate 22. The Roman Villa, Rabat: the mosaic impluvium in the atrium

Downstairs, the main room was the *atrium* of the Roman house, the central court with peristyle around. The basin at the centre, the impluvium, is floored with a charming, if rather hackneyed, mosaic of birds drinking from a bowl (Plate 22), enclosed within a *trompe-l'œil* 'relief' maze pattern. Rain water caught in it was channelled into the cistern below the southern corner. Some of the fallen blocks of the portico have been restored to their original position, and the rest reconstructed to match.

Opening off the atrium to the south-west are two smaller rooms, the reception rooms of this luxurious town house, both with mosaics. In one the floor was restored several times in antiquity, though not, be it admitted, very well. The other was the *triclinium*, or main dining-room. Its mosaic was of far higher quality, delicate work with minute tesserae, but this has not survived well. Its central panel has been lifted and attached to the wall of the atrium. The panel is an easel piece in a

Plate 23. The Roman Villa, Rabat: the problematical figured mosaic

carved stone tray perhaps representing Summer, a child with flowers and fruits. Alongside it is an even finer, if more controversial, one. This is a much more ambitious scene including a female and a bound male figure—Omphale and Hercules? Delilah and Samson (they look very like scissors she is holding)? or some other pair altogether? The technique is Pergamene, but the stone trays—an empty one stands on the ground near—appear to be of local rock, suggesting an itinerant artist. We remember the lyre player from the same city whose tombstone is upstairs.

Luxury is also implied by the life-size marble statues standing around the triclinium, close to their original find spots. Their damaged state prevents our identifying their subjects.

The first case on the north-east wall has photographs and finds of the site on Ras ir-Raħeb (p. 127), including intriguing terracotta figurine fragments and a delicate carved bone relief of a kneeling boar. The next long case shows some of the finds from the villa itself—various pottery fragments, mainly of early imperial date, and scraps of bronze, iron, glass, etc. The third case deals with the round tower of Ta' Ġawhar (p. 89). Noteworthy here are the little gold ear-ring and the carbonized bread roll, both treasures in their different ways. Beside it is the stone block from the same site, carved in a 1st-century style and built into the tower in the later 2nd or 3rd century. It crashed into the ruins when the tower burnt down at the end of the 3rd century, and lay there until excavated in 1960.

Further along this wall are mementoes of the last period of use of the Roman Villa site, a graphic illustration of the shrinking of the city in the Dark Ages. In the Arab period, when the defences of Mdina were redrawn on their present lines, the ruins beyond became a convenient cemetery area. These tombstones, many with Koranic texts in the monumental Kufic script, were set up all over the site, wherever graves had been dug into the Roman town house. This use too ceased when medieval Christianity decreed church burial.

The Phoenician, Punic and Roman cemeteries similarly lay outside the town of their period. On three sides, the city's limits were clearly marked by the slope. On the fourth, parts of the Roman boundary ditch remain traceable in several places through Rabat. A cul-de-sac on the right of Nikol Saura Street (leading to Buskett and Dingli) 50 metres from the Saqqaja Square marks its line. St Paul's Grotto under the parish church is a cave in the side of the ditch where Paul is said to have passed some of his captivity, though this is not mentioned in our only

8

source, the Acts of the Apostles. The new road in front of the church again follows the line of the ditch to the northern scarp edge.

Immediately beyond the church, which must be on or very near one of the main gates of the Roman town, the cemeteries begin. Early tombs have been found particularly out along Ferris Street in the Kola Xagħra and Taċ-Ċagħqi areas. A small catacomb is still accessible under the school here. But the main catacombs, those of St Catald, St Paul and St Agatha, and there are many smaller ones, are to be found along the next road.

The largest group, the so-called *St Paul's Catacombs*, are in government ownership and form a popular tourist attraction.

A steep flight of steps is cut into the rock, with small *loculus* graves for children in either side. At the foot of the stairs, one is confronted by a pillar left in the solid rock. To the left of it, at a slightly lower level, is the room interpreted as the chapel (Fig. 21). An altar reported by early writers has since disappeared. To the left of this chapel, a grave has been restored with material from elsewhere; the catacombs themselves were despoiled many centuries ago.

On the other side of the pillar is another imposing hall, obviously the centre of the whole monument. At either end is a so-called *agape* table, a common feature in the Maltese catacombs. It consists of a circular table, carved from the rock, with a bench at the same level on all sides except where a niche allows direct access to the table. This is thought to have been for the funeral feast or wake, part of the ceremony of final leave-taking. Scratched into the roof of this hall can be made out crosses and coats of arms, probably souvenirs of visitors in the Knights' period.

Passages lead off from these halls in several directions into the bewildering galleries of tombs. In two places, as marked on the plan, traces of inscriptions in red on the white rock or plaster can be seen. The first is still legible—EVTYXION (Eutychion). The seated figure once visible beside it can hardly be made out any longer. Such frescoing was presumably once universal throughout these catacombs, giving details, perhaps even representations, of the deceased in every grave. And the main halls were almost certainly once suitably decorated. But these faint scraps are all that survive.

A plan of the galleries is given, so a detailed description is unnecessary. It remains, however, to describe the main types of tomb (Fig. 22). The *loculus* has already been mentioned. This is the simplest form, a rectangular box cut in the wall. A rebate allowed tiles to be cemented across the opening. Many are small, the resting place of children. Next

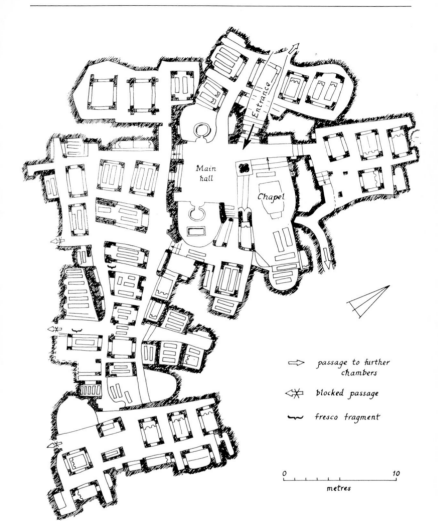

Fig. 21. St. Paul's Catacombs, Rabat

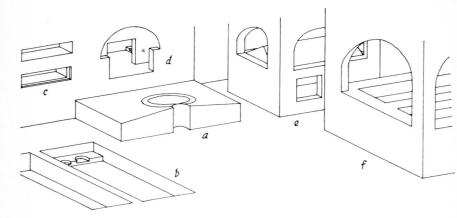

Fig. 22. The principal types of grave in the Maltese catacombs: *a* agape table; *b* floor graves, one with head-rest; *c* loculus graves; *d* arcosolium tomb; *e* saddle-backed canopied tomb; *f* ordinary canopied tomb

comes the type of tomb consisting of a rectangular pit cut into the rock of the floor. Some are single, as in the floor of the chapel, some multiple, but the great majority in pairs. The finest are the canopied table graves, where a pair of these tombs at waist height have arched openings between the pillars which connect their corners to the roof. All these graves would have been sealed individually with tiles or stone slabs. A variant of the last is the saddle-backed canopied tomb, in which the surface at waist level is carved as a lid or roof. A chamber is cut beneath this, entered from the side. The carved headrests show that it was still intended for two bodies, presumably husband and wife. A simpler variant of this has an identical chamber carved in the side wall, the square entrance opening from a semicircular niche, often with carved pilasters. This *arcosolium* type occurs in some of the minor catacombs, but there are no good examples in the main part of the St Paul's Catacombs.

This group, indeed, is only one, if the largest, of a large number of catacombs in the area, several of them cutting into each other, so honeycombed is the rock. Of the twenty-five government owned ones here and in the nursery garden on the other side of the road, only a few require special mention. No. 3 has on one of its blocking slabs a relief carving of weaving tools, implying that it belonged to a guild of weavers. Nos. 10, 12, 13 and 14 form a group belonging to a Jewish community, as shown by the *tora*, the seven-branched candlestick, carved on their walls. No. 10 is further distinguished by still having the stone door of one of its side chambers, now re-erected. It swings somewhat gratingly on a pivot and socket, hinges being of course out of the question in stone. No. 17 is one of the best preserved.

St Agatha's Catacombs, under the church a little further out, are another extensive group. Arcosolium tombs are much better represented here, and the cemetery chapel was refounded and refrescoed in medieval times.

The same applies to the *Abbatija tad-Dejr Catacombs*. These are on the left of the road which forks on the other side of the chapel of St Catald. The key is kept at a shop alongside its entrance from the road. Besides the chapel, this group is noteworthy for frescoed relief decoration inside the roof of some of its canopied tombs. The cross occurs here too, in contrast to the dearth of Christian symbolism in the Rabat catacombs as a whole. For the more important field catacombs, see pp. 132, 76, 88 (Salina, San Tumas, Ħal Resqun).

The cemetery area extended much further out. There are tombs and catacombs in the cliffs around Tal Virtu for example, the second promontory south of Rabat towards Buskett. Many of the museum exhibits are from tombs in the Għajn Klieb/Għajn Qajjet area, either side of the road 1·5 kilometres west of Rabat. The Mtarfa ridge might be regarded as a city of the dead over against the city of the living, as on many Etruscan sites—though no reflection is intended on the service hospital and barracks which now stand on the site. Particularly worthy of comment are the Phoenician tombs which cut through cart-ruts running along the neck of the promontory just west of the hospital grounds. Bronze Age material was recovered from silo pits nearer the tip, and there is a tradition, unfortunately unsubstantiated, of a classical temple having occupied this site.

The direct road back to Rabat drops steeply from Mtarfa to cross the valley floor on a rather surprising causeway. The explanation will be found where the road begins the climb on the Rabat side. The building here could only have been a railway station. It was indeed the terminus of the Malta Railway until the line was closed in 1931. To the east, the line passed beneath Mdina in a tunnel, now a flourishing mushroom farm. The track was extended to the foot of Mtarfa to serve as a military link with the harbour area.

BUSKETT AND DINGLI

Southward from Rabat the plateau rises gently to just over 250 metres, and then plunges precipitately into the sea. The road along the cliff top, approached from Rabat via Dingli or Buskett, and from Siġġiewi via Girgenti, is justly famous for its scenery. The sheltered eastward-facing valleys of Buskett and Girgenti have been appreciated even longer.

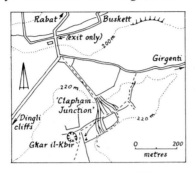

Fig. 23. The cart-ruts at 'Clapham Junction' and the Għar il-Kbir, Buskett

Grand Master Verdala in 1586 built himself a summer residence at the first, and laid out extensive citrus groves in the valley below. A little over a kilometre to the south-east, out of sight but probably rarely out of mind, the Grand Inquisitor too had his summer palace, smaller and more intimate, a delightful retreat after his gaunt palace in Vittoriosa.

The major antiquities of this region lie immediately south of the *Buskett Gardens* (Fig. 23). At the end of the gardens, the cliff road crosses the head of the Buskett (or Boschetto) valley at a crossroads (left, exit only, from the gardens, right to Dingli), and just beyond forks right. The rough road to the left descends ultimately to Siġġiewi. The footpath bisecting the angle between the fork climbs for 200 metres to a broad concave slope of rock, bare but for small pockets of earth caught in its irregularities, which in the spring are rich with flowers.

The popular name of *Clapham Junction* refers to the dense concentration of cart-ruts which fan out from this point to cross the ridge ahead in the direction of the upper Girgenti valley beyond. One pair runs along the crest of the ridge to intersect all the rest. A full plan of these has recently been attempted, and may eventually show how many pairs of ruts can be distinguished. It must run to several score. This is the most impressive group of ruts on the island, offering a challenge to the imagination of every visitor.

Plate 24. Buskett: the cart-ruts of 'Clapham Junction' (*above*) and Għar il-Kbir, with the Buskett Gardens and Verdala Palace beyond (*below*)

The clearest part of the group lies over the crest to the right of the central field (Plate 24). The stone wall bounding the open rock offers a convenient vantage point for photographers. Near the western wall here, square Punic tomb shafts can be seen, one of which cuts through a rut, so proving the rut's greater antiquity.

Following the ridge towards the south-west will bring the visitor to the crater-like *Għar il-Kbir* (Plate 24). Indeed, the transverse rut mentioned above is interrupted by its lip, but priority cannot be held as proven here, since this may be the effect of a subsequent rock fall. The cave itself, the name means simply 'the big cave', should surely be classed as another of the sights of Malta. The easiest entrance is at the southern corner. Do not be discouraged by the strong smell of goat, the only modern inhabitants.

The cave's origin is obviously similar to that of the Maqluba at Qrendi (p. 93), a large dissolution pocket in the rock, of which the roof at some time collapsed. How early the caves and rock overhangs in its walls were used for human settlement is not known. The longer a cave remains in occupation, the less the chance of survival of ancient deposits on its floor. What is known is the date at which habitation ceased—1835. In that year, the British administration resettled the residents, against their wishes, in Siġġiewi, considering their cave home far too insanitary for human occupation. Fortunately the German artist Brocktorff (see also p. 153) painted the scene for us shortly before. One cannot but sympathize with the government officials.

Beyond this area, a famous one for its orchids in late spring, there are several antiquities of lesser importance, still worthy of note. The eastern tip of the plateau above Siġġiewi (lane east from the Girgenti road beside the quarry, or a steep footpath up from the sharp bend in the Siġġiewi–Fawwara road) bears two chapels and the great Laferla Cross. The views over the lower half of the island are noteworthy. South of the lane by the San Lawrenz chapel is more rock with ruts, including the best evidence for soil erosion since they were cut. One prominent pair sets out to cross the rock expanse, becoming progressively shallower until they clip only the highest reefs of stone, and then vanish completely. There seems to be a straight choice here between accepting that a soil layer has since been swept away, or that the carts themselves became airborne.

At the south-east end of the cliff road, where it swings inland at Ta' Żuta towards Girgenti, a lane descends to the rocky promontory of the *Wardija ta' San Ġorġ*. The surrounding cliffs, and a plentiful water supply at their foot, attracted settlement in the Bronze Age. Traces of masonry across the neck, a bell-shaped silo pit in the rock, and a scatter of sherds testify to a walled village like that of Borġ in-Nadur itself. The lane continues by a series of hairpins, at the time of writing not recommended for wheeled vehicles, to Fawwara below the cliffs. Here there is a copious spring breaking out above the clay, one of the island's principal sources of water at the present day. A large cave nearby has been much altered by man, removing all traces of early occupation in the process. The niches may have been cut to hold Roman cremation urns, making it a *columbarium*.

Another more open Bronze Age settlement must once have stood on the lip of the cliff a kilometre to the north-west. No trace survives on the bare rock, but Mallia has recovered rich material in recent years from the rock fissures of Għar Mirdum below the cliff, where it was presumably thrown from above.

Ruts follow closely the cliff road between the Buskett turn and the Madalena Chapel. One faint one runs off the cliff edge and another makes a short very steep climb. Better examples of both phenomena will be noted later (pp. 139 and 126). Just west of the radio masts which mark the highest point on the island, 252 metres, and on the opposite side of the road, two loose boulders appear to be the last remains of some megalithic structure, judging by a few temple period sherds which have been found around them. It is perhaps surprising that anything has survived from this exposed spot.

BAĦRIJA

The north-west corner of the plateau is served by a number of roads radiating from Rabat, starting from beside the Roman villa. They are well signposted. The first fork is beside the pumping station at Għajn Klieb, 1·6 kilometres west of Rabat. To the west of the station are the scanty remains of a round tower (see in particular p. 89), obviously guarding the western approaches of the Roman capital. The Mtaħleb road forks left here, and left again just beyond the Fiddien Bridge. Just before it climbs steeply out of the valley, yet another left fork, an unsignposted lane, leads in a kilometre to the cliff hamlet of *Għar Żerrieq*, overlooking the very attractive Wied ir-Rum. There are fine ruts on the cliff lip, including the best example of one cut by cliff falls (Plate 25).

Plate 25. Cart-ruts on the lip of the cliff at Għar Żerrieq (*above*); Mtaħleb and the Wied ta' Miġra Ferħa (*below*). Note the cave-dwelling in the bottom left-hand corner

A pleasant track follows the cliff lip round to *Mtaħleb*, reached more directly by the mainer road from the last fork. This is another picturesque cliff village of unknown antiquity (Plate 25). Some of the houses are true cave-dwellings behind their built façades. Megaliths are reported from time to time on the hills below the cliff here, but they are natural, the fragmented remains of the upper coralline limestone capping which once covered them. The valley which separates them from the higher ground, the Wied ta' Miġra Ferħa, was the route by which Count Roger in 1090 led his successful attack on the Arabs. One can still scramble down to sea level, where swimming with a snorkel mask—calm weather is essential—is more than spectacular. The cliffs rise 30 metres above the surface and plunge another 20 below.

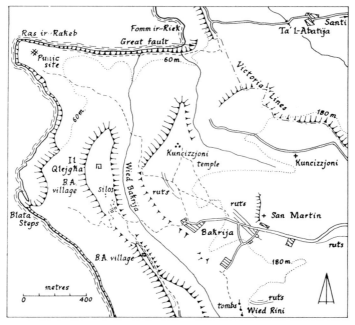

Fig. 24. The archaeological sites around Baħrija

A lane from Mtaħleb follows the cliff to the right for 3 kilometres, passing poor cart-ruts and some Punic tomb shafts, to Il Qlejgħa ta' Baħrija, see below. Cars can negotiate the first 2 kilometres.

Plate 26. Baħrija, the Bronze Age village site of Il Qlejgħa, with the cliffs of Gozo in the distance

The right fork at the Fiddien Bridge gives one, after another mile, a choice of three forks, to San Martin, Kunċizzjoni and Santi. *San Martin* is a hamlet (Fig. 24) grouped round an expanse of bare rock with more ruts on it. Indeed, the bar on the south of the road has a fine pair apparently entering its front door. They reappear under its back wall. The road continues a further 350 metres to stop on the cliff edge at *Baħrija*. The track opposite the shop plunges over the cliff and down to the Wied Baħrija. This is an unexpected corner, particularly in the height of summer, because of its running water, greenery, dragonflies, frogs and, startling if you have not been warned of them, freshwater crabs. The path then climbs, in 45 minutes from the road, to the final ridge before the sea, on which stood Malta's most impressive Bronze Age village.

Il Qlejgħa ta' Baħrija, to give it its full name, is a crescent-shaped plateau tilted to the east (Plate 26). It is 700 metres long by some 200 wide. Its westward cliff tops 170 metres. The whole of this promontory was occupied by the village: sherds are freely scattered across the terraced fields, in several places bell-shaped water cisterns or silo pits can be seen cut in the solid rock, and two deep stone mortars for grain pounding have been recorded, built into modern field walls. There are no traces of built defences here, and indeed they would have been superfluous. Eric Peet in 1908 put in some trenches, yielding rich pottery of what Evans (p. 48) came to call the Baħrija phase. Another trench in 1959 showed Borġ in-Nadur material stratified below this.

From the northern tip, one gets a good view of the remotest corner of the island, Ras ir-Raħeb, but direct access is not possible (see p. 127). Gozo stands along the horizon beyond. But it is the vast area of sea which impresses most, with a great unbroken sweep 180° from Gozo to Dingli. Within that curve the surface mirrors the day's weather, ruffled or white-horsed, catspawed or, very rarely, dead calm, according to the wind, and blue or near-black, shot-silk or dappled, according to the clouds. On that horizon on an exceptionally haze-free evening I have once seen the green flash left by the sun at the moment of setting.

A path from the southern end of the plateau descends to the sea by the Blata Steps, artificially cut and probably of comparatively recent date. The next crest to the south is barren, but the second, a much smaller flat plateau, also has Bronze Age sherds, of the Borġ in-Nadur type, and one circular rock-cut house foundation. Access is easiest from its southern tip. It gives an excellent viewpoint for the Baħrija site, and indeed much of north-western Malta and a substantial part of Gozo too. It is difficult here to believe in Malta's 300,000 population.

From the road-head at Baħrija, another path runs due north through the last farmyard, then bears left down a steep slope to cross the Wied Baħrija opposite the tip of Il Qlejgħa. It continues round the foot of that site to Ras ir-Raħeb (p. 127), a longer walk (about 1½ hours) but less nerve-racking than the brinkmanship of the path from Fomm ir-Rieħ.

Accessible from this path before it drops into the Wied is another temple site, Li Mdawra or more usually *Kunċizzjoni*, so-called from the chapel of the Immaculate Conception (via the Italian Concezzione) on the next road. The site, dug in 1938, is not an impressive one and yielded an irregular plan. It is some 200 metres south of where the D.O.S. map places it. The chapel is worth mention for its ship graffiti, but for a description of better ones see p. 86. The right-hand road from back at the fork leads to the Santi Gap (p. 128), and so down to Mġarr.

Back at Għajn Klieb, the right-hand fork (ignore the Għemieri road, which has no exit) crosses the valley at Tas-Salib above the Chadwick Lakes (a series of 19th-century reservoirs, dry through most of the year) and climbs to the Bengemma Gap (p. 129). A typical Maltese farmhouse stands on the ridge at the top of the first steep climb. The slope below, out on the east of the road, *Qalillija*, is well worth exploring for its ruts. It is quite a steep slope, and at one point, quite near the road, ruts climb a projecting reef of rock at an angle of 45°, one in one, for 1·40 metres. Here the problem of what powered the 'carts' is at its most acute.

At the top of the next climb and just beyond another farm (note the pair of cow horns set up to ward off the evil eye) are more ruts, a good junction on the right and a sweeping curve on the left. Here they are clearly cut by the square shaft of one of a group of Punic tombs. Northwards, the ruts swing round the slope towards the Nadur Tower.

Immediately beside the road opposite the junction is a tomb with a round shaft, the one which produced the Ġgantija phase pottery in the National Museum, p. 43, and so the oldest shaft-and-chamber tomb yet to come to light.

5 · NORTH MALTA

THE GREAT FAULT AND VICTORIA LINES

As mentioned in the geographical section at the beginning (p. 18), a major feature of Malta's structure is the fault which crosses the island from west to east, from Ras ir-Raħeb to the Madalena Tower. The clearest place to see it is at the head of Fomm ir-Rieħ (the Mouth of the Wind—you have been warned!) Bay. A lane, recently surfaced, runs west from the Santi road past Tal Abbatija to this point. The sheer cliffs on the south of the bay, of lower coralline limestone, form the face of the fault. The softer globigerina and clay brought down level with them have eroded away along the line of weakness. If one takes the track to the south, and then descends the small valley to the lip of these cliffs, the fault is clearly visible in section to one's right.

An exciting walk, requiring a good head for heights and a calm day, is provided by the footpath along the cliff top, 45 metres sheer above the sea, to the headland of *Ras ir-Raħeb*. A longer but less vertiginous path descends from San Martin (p. 125), crossing the Wied Baħrija. This must surely be the remotest corner of the island, and likely to remain so. But it was not always as empty as it is now. There are extensive remains of a large building with a central courtyard. An adjoining room is floored with diamond-shaped tiles and a large rectangular cistern is cut in the rock beneath. A quantity of puzzling material (p. 113) was recovered from here in 1963, showing a mixture of Punic and Roman influence and suggesting a date in about the 1st century B.C. or A.D. though this is far from secure. Even the nature of the building is unsure since erosion has left so little of the plan, let alone the contemporary deposits. It could have been either a religious site or a rich country retreat. The courtyard shows some similarity to that of Tas-Silġ.

Eastwards from Fomm ir-Rieħ, the fault itself is masked by erosion. The upper coralline cliffs, as at Baħrija above Ras ir-Raħeb, continue as the scarp of the Benġemma Hills, but well to the south of the actual fault line.

The *Victoria Lines* were built in the 1880s, when the British Empire was at cross purposes with two other world powers, France and Russia. The idea behind them was that the fault escarpment offered a more economic defence line than the remote and much indented shore of north Malta, with its many convenient landing-places. This strategy is perhaps debatable, emphasizing as it does the importance of the harbours as a base for the Royal Navy, but ignoring the Navy's capabilities for its own defence at sea. Be that as it may, the lines consist of a series of forts, connected by a continuous breastwork with a dry ditch cut in front wherever it was considered necessary.

The line climbs directly from the head of Fomm ir-Rieħ Bay to the upper scarp, but is poorly preserved where it crosses the unstable and heavily cultivated blue clay. Beyond that, it sticks to the upper cliffs as far as the main Mosta-Mġarr road, with Forts Benġemma and Dwejra in its length. There are two routes across it in this stretch. The *Santi Gap* has the ruin of a Roman round tower like Ta' Ġawhar across the valley from the present road, which suggests that this route was in use as early as Roman times.

Plate 27. Benġemma; from left to right the chapel of Madonna tal-Lettera, with a cave below, two pairs of crossing cart-ruts, Mġarr church, and the ditch and wall of the Victoria Lines. The late Roman cemetery is in the valley below the last.

The *Benġemma Gap*, still a steep and difficult road, had the Knights' Nadur Tower to keep a watch on it. It was in use even earlier, as shown by cart-ruts descending into it immediately to the east of the little chapel of the Madonna tal-Lettera (Plate 27). (Santi has ruts too, but they appear to skirt the valley head rather than descend it.) No Roman defensive work is known here. Instead there is an extensive cemetery, associated perhaps with a settlement either under the modern farm or down the hill on the site of the present hamlet of Benġemma. A large number of small catacombs are cut in the walls of the little valley below the chapel, both inside and outside the Lines. The niches in the cliff by the farm may be another *columbarium*, for Roman cremation urns. The Victoria Lines themselves remain the main feature of the district, this being one of their most impressive and easily accessible stretches.

The *Falka Gap* offers the easiest means of crossing the fault scarp. Here the upper coralline has been completely removed, leaving an open shelf before the lower coralline, and the fault itself, outcrop again towards Tarġa. The knights plugged this gap with the Torri Falka and a line of entrenchments, built by Grand Master Perellos in the 17th century. A cave below the tower produced a small amount of temple period pottery, though there is nothing to suggest defences of that period. The gap was certainly used in the Bronze Age, with a few ruts surviving on the south side of the modern road despite the softer rock of the area.

The *Tarġa Gap* road has the appearance of being of quite recent date. 'Gap' is certainly a misnomer here as the road has to make a great hair-pin to negotiate the steep slope. The cliffs form the main fault face again. The small catacomb just east of the Rabat road a hundred metres south of the main road need not, of course, imply a through route. A finer catacomb in level ground within *Fort Mosta* (special permission is required to visit this) certainly cannot imply anything of the sort, as the only approach is along the ridge from the south-west. This makes the fort, the hinge of the whole lines, look a very suitable site for a Bronze Age settlement. No sherds have been recorded to support this, due one imagines to the combined effects of erosion and military engineering. Bare rock to the west shows cart-ruts heading for the point, with further progress barred by the cliffs, a situation like that at many of the known villages of this date.

The biggest hole through the fault scarp is that cut by the *Wied tal-Isperanza* after its waters, instead of emptying down the now dry valley through Birkirkara to Marsamxett, breached the Benġemma–

9

Naxxar ridge to flow out to Salina. But the valley is a steep-sided gorge, delightful for a country stroll (note particularly the chapel built into a cave below Fort Mosta) or for practice in rock-climbing, but little suitable for through traffic. The Lines bar it with a massive wall, with patrolway and breastwork on its crest.

On the ridge between the Wied tal-Isperanza and the next, minor, valley to the east, the *Wied Filep*, a very good example of a Maltese dolmen can be seen. It lies immediately behind the first field wall south of, and in the angle of, the Mosta–Naxxar Gap road. This area is another noted for its wild flowers.

The *Naxxar Gap*, below *San Pawl tat-Targa* (St Paul of the Stair-case), is another straight-scarp one, this time with plentiful evidence of ancient use in the shape of a magnificent series of cart-ruts. These approach the Victoria Lines generally from the south, crossing the Mosta road on a broad front. In the road verges are some of the deepest recorded, cutting 24 inches into the rock. The ruts then swing parallel to, or even under, the main road and turn again to go down the gentle ridge towards the south-south-west. The 1939 pillbox at the first bend in the road, successor to the Torri tal-Kaptan up the hill in San Pawl, makes a good landmark. A hundred metres or so down the slope, the ruts fork. Some continue on the same line until they swing gradually to the right, to disappear under fields by the chapel of Santa Katerina. It is probably this group which reappears a kilometre away at Tal Qraj (p. 133) and continues to Salina. The second group takes a remarkably sharp bend back to the north-east, to vanish under the road again in the direction of Maghtab.

A cistern has been cut to take the run-off from one of these ruts, but this is clearly a subsequent feature. Though they are difficult to explain as vehicle tracks (note in particular some very steep steps on this slope), they cannot possibly be accepted as water catchment schemes, at least as their primary function. The universal pairing of them is only one of many contrary arguments.

On the next stretch, the cliffs again represent the actual fault face, though there are two incised gorges, the Wieds Anglu and Faham, for the Victoria Lines to negotiate. The extraordinary red camouflaged structure in the fields below deserves passing note as a defence of a different kind. It is 'The Ear', built in 1940 to concentrate the sound of enemy planes revving up for take-off in Sicily for the benefit of a sensi-tive microphone at its centre. Surprising though it may seem in view of the 95 kilometre distance, it worked, to give a very welcome warning of impending air raids.

Fort Madalena, on the last spur of the Naxxar–Gharghur heights, was sited to hold the coastal flank. The present coast road is of recent construction, before which there was only the country lane from Maghtab. Even so, this flank required something more than the simple breastwork which sufficed in the difficult terrain on the west coast. The Madalena Tower illustrates the Knights' anxieties over the same point.

THE SALINA DISTRICT

Beyond the Great Fault, the north of the island has much more varied scenery than the east, largely brought about by a series of lesser fault lines running approximately east–west. The result is a succession of ridges and valleys tilted by later earth movement to form cliffs on the west and low shores, the valleys often flooded, on the east. This region was very sparsely inhabited until the threat of raids by corsairs declined in the 18th century, and the thicker sprinkle of ancient sites may be due more to this than to any original pattern of settlement.

The eastern end of this block differs markedly from the rest. First comes a group of low hills with several sites around its flanks. It is best approached by the coast road on its north. From this, a lane turns inland at the head of the second bay, the Qala San Marku, to the district known as *Il Maghtab*. 250 metres from the main road, on a ledge of rock on the right, can be seen the *Ta' Hammut* dolmens. The first is the best preserved, a slab of rock so low to the ground that only a scoop in the rock beneath it gave the space for even cremation burials. It was in this scoop that Professor Evans in 1954 found the sherds which dated this class of monument to the Early Bronze Age. The rock slabs of at least two more dolmens survive within the next few metres.

Higher on the slope, just west of a farmhouse and 200 metres from the dolmens, the remains of another temple period building, though not of standard plan, can be seen among the carobs.

This north coast has a fine series of the Knights' defensive towers: Madalena, Qalet Marku, Ghallis and Qawra either side of the mouth of *Salina Bay*, and so to the oldest of them (1610), which now serves as St Paul's Bay telephone exchange. At the head of Salina were further defences, a redoubt and a fougasse at either side. The fougasse is best described as a rock-cut cannon, with a bore of nearly 2 metres. It was charged with gunpowder and loose rocks and fired by means of a fuse the groove for which is still visible. The one beside the eastern Salina redoubt is the best preserved, and it is rumoured that it was kept loaded during the early part of the last war. It was aimed to scatter rocks along the eastern shore of the bay, whilst its partner covered the western side. Its use might well have made the difference between a successful and an unsuccessful hostile landing, though in the event none has been attempted since its cutting in the 17th century. Many bays at that time were so protected.

Salina is named after the salt pans still in use at the head of the bay, and there is a smaller set cut in the rock of its western shore. They were built early in the Knights' period to replace a more exposed set in Mellieħa Bay. Long before this, Salina had a different economic importance. The number of finds of Roman lead anchors (see p. 49), pottery, etc. from the sea floor suggests that at that time it served as a small port.

Local wealth is also implied by a group of catacombs close to the lane behind the Annunziata chapel. The first has two arched chambers, a moulding round one of the arches terminating in spiral ends. The second catacomb is much larger and indeed once had a central hall, but this was almost entirely cut away in quarrying the stone for building the nearby chapel. Three passages of tomb chambers survive, that on the south, with a well-preserved *agape* table, being the most extensive. The third catacomb is the most important. It lies a few metres to the north, at the back of the upper terrace. It is protected by an iron gate, the key to which can be borrowed from the National Museum.

Its doorway had some architectural pretensions, carved pilasters and a triangular tympanum above it. Within, the passage has an *agape* table on its left and three magnificent canopy tombs beside and beyond it. There are carved pilasters, spiral mouldings, and occasional relief symbols, all cut from the solid rock. Each tomb has space for, and head-rests for, two occupants. Did no Maltese Romans die single, or twice married? The impression is of a small but wealthy family, its successive heads, and their spouses, occupying the central tombs, their brothers and cousins the simpler chambers in the side passages. Were they Christians? One of the symbols is a cross within a circle, making it likely but not absolutely certain. Another, on the left wall as you reach the entrance again, shows an outline stag with spreading horns. This is known as an early symbol for divine grace, but is still hardly conclusive.

Beside the Annunziata Chapel can be made out more of the mysterious cart-ruts. They can be traced round the slope of the hill intermittently for 1·5 kilometres by which time they are clearly heading for the foot of the San Pawl tat-Tarġa group (p. 130). Together, these make as good economic sense as any in the island, connecting undiscovered settlements on the Naxxar–Għargħur hill tops with the sea at Salina, whence would be brought salt, fish and perhaps seaweed as fertilizer.

Seven hundred metres south of the palm trees at the end of the saltpans, and set well above the modern lane and ancient ruts, is the temple of *Tal Qadi* (Tal Qraj on older maps). Here for once the topography has overruled the temple builders' preference for an axis pointing between east and south. Enough of the plan can be made out to show an axis facing straight down the slope to the south-west, and at the time of the excavation in 1927 this was even clearer. It is a very pleasant site, dropping to the fertile plain of Burmarrad and across to the Great Fault, Ġebel Għawżara and Wardija.

Very different, particularly now, is the temple at *Buġibba* on the St Paul's Bay side of the Buġibba peninsula. Only 6 metres above sea level, it turns its back on the sea and the beauties of the bay to face across a low and uninteresting slope. It had a neat trefoil plan and some decorated blocks, one of them, with relief fish (p. 49), unique. The site has now been engulfed by the incorrectly named Dolmen Hotel, a building in a modern Maltese style which tries to echo that of the prehistoric temples.

The last site in this area again overlooks the Burmarrad plain, but this time from the western slopes, immediately above the Wardija crossroads. This is the Roman site of *San Pawl Milqgħi*, St Paul Welcomed, the traditional site of Paul's first meeting with Publius, the island's Roman governor. The key is kept at the National Museum. Excavations by the Italian Missione Archeologica in Malta in 1963–8 have revealed the extent and history of the site. A large agricultural establishment was founded here in the 2nd century B.C., but was destroyed by fire in the early 1st century A.D. It was refounded on an even larger scale and flourished in the 4th–5th century. The main activity was clearly the extraction of olive oil, as the pippers, settling tanks, etc. show. The present chapel was built between 1616 and 1622, but there are traces of earlier ones on the site and a documentary record of 1488.

The unsettled question is the identification with Publius's villa. Although this was a dwelling site as well as an industrial one—painted

wall plaster was found for example—it is far more modest than one
would expect of a governor's country villa. Paul would have been here
about A.D. 60, after the first destruction but, if the interim report has
been understood aright, well before the second active period on the
site. Scattered Christian symbols of this later date are hardly relevant.
The word ΠΑVΛVS engraved roughly on one of the blocks at the same
late date helps little. Another engraving of a man is inconclusive, being
unnamed and accompanied not by a ship but by two ships, which seem
difficult to reconcile with the story. The matter must be considered for
the moment unproven, though the archaeological importance of the site
for the economics of Roman Malta remains unchallenged.

The rest of north Malta is divided topographically by the ridge-and-
valley belts which are so prominent a feature of its scenery. The first
north of the Great Fault is the Benġemma valley and *Bidnija Ridge*. The
ridge begins at Ġebel Għawżara, immediately above San Pawl Milqghi.
A Bronze Age settlement is suspected here, but is as yet unconfirmed.
A typical Bronze Age site occupies the next hilltop to the west, Il
Qolla. This is a cliff-girt promontory between branches of the Wied

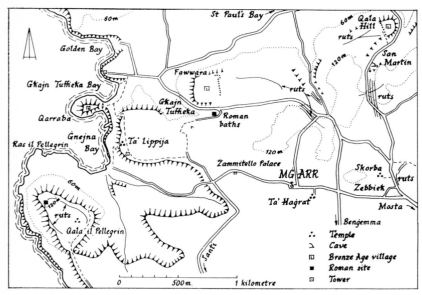

Fig. 25. Mġarr and its sites

Qannotta, clearly visible from the main road at the Wardija crossroads, and indeed from the sea at Salina. Apart from a few undistinguished cart-ruts, there is nothing from antiquity until one reaches the Għajn Tuffieħa road at Żebbieħ (Fig. 25).

Here a group of ruts runs close to the modern road immediately north of the hamlet. The rocky field to the right contains some rectangular Puno-Roman tomb shafts, now blocked. On the left, a lane runs 50 metres west to the site of Li Skorba.

SKORBA

The importance of this site lies less in the upstanding remains than in the information the excavations here in 1960–3 gave on the temple period, and even more on the pre-temple period.

The heart of the site is a typical 3-apse temple of the Ġgantija phase, of which the greater part of the first two apses and the whole of the façade had already been destroyed to ground level. What remain here are the stone paving of the entrance passage, with its perforations to carry libation offerings, the *torba* floors of the apses, and by some fluke of survival one of the megalithic uprights, a 3·40 metre high slab of coralline limestone. *Torba*, it should be explained, is a cement-like flooring material made from the local globigerina by crushing, watering and pounding. In the paving, particularly of the right apse, can be seen some of the internal fittings, a step once covered with pitted decoration, a porthole niche and two trilithon altars against the rear walls.

The north wall is in much better shape. Originally the entrance was open to the court, as in the southern temple at the Ġgantija, but in the Tarxien phase it was closed off with a wall and doorway, and altars were set into the corners so formed. Later still, when the building was already ruinous, rougher masonry walls were added inside the apse to turn it into a humble dwelling of the first Bronze Age phase. Dating for these structural alterations is provided by the pottery fragments associated with each, as discovered during excavation.

The boundary wall of the temple is less impressive again because the building had been cut into sloping deposits of earlier date. All we see is the lowest course of the foundations, the free-standing superstructure having long since gone. The natural slope continues to the south, where a terraced forecourt was supported by a wall nearly 2 metres high. Part of the original masonry is incorporated into the modern terrace wall in the south-west corner of the field.

Immediately to the west of the temple, and built against it, were two small additional rooms. The first still had a patch of red painted plaster clinging to its wall when exposed, and its floor too was ochred all over. But both these rooms had gone out of use and been filled with rubbish before the end of the temple period. There may once have been other rooms filling the angle to the terrace wall but now destroyed by cultivation.

East of this temple, a second was added in the Tarxien phase, with four apses and a central niche. It was in a more ruinous state when found and was indeed probably less well built in the first place. It is further obscured by the right of way, which had to be restored after the excavation, across its inner apse. The breaks in its *torba* floor were not made by clumsy excavators but by local farmers wishing to bury dead livestock where the soil was deep enough to cover them adequately. Rubbish on the floors below the remains of the burnt roof implied that this temple went out of use before its neighbour. The megalithic blocks in the angle of the lane were probably an external shrine at the end of the façade, like the better-preserved examples at Tarxien.

Before the temples were built, this slope had supported a flourishing village over a period of some twelve centuries. Though much of the evidence was necessarily cut away by the temple builders, extensive deposits remained on all sides. The oldest structure is the 11 metre long straight wall to the west of the first temple's entrance. The deposit against it contained material of the first known human occupation of the island, the Għar Dalam phase, and charcoal which gave two radio-carbon dates, one either side of 4000 B.C. It also yielded important information on the domestic animals (sheep, goats and cattle) and cultivated crops (barley, emmer and club wheat, lentils) of these early settlers.

Behind the temple outbuildings, a rectangular hut floor can be seen, immediately preceding the temple in date. It had been burnt down, burying a useful collection of Ġgantija phase pottery in its collapse. Trenches to its east, behind the temple, gave invaluable successions of the different pottery styles used on the site, two of which had not been recognized before the excavation here began.

In the field east of the eastern temple, a much more extensive structure came to light, belonging to the Red Skorba phase, with C[14] dates around 3300 B.C. Two rooms should perhaps be considered base-ments as the southern one had no doorway through its massive walls. The northern one was entered from a pebbled court which could not be pursued beneath the east temple. The irregularity of the floors, the unlevelled surface of bedrock, argues against a domestic use, and the group of figurines in the National Museum from the northern room also suggests that this building had a religious function, a true predecessor, then, of the temples which first appeared some centuries later.

MĠARR

One does not have to go far for the next temple, which lies at the entrance to the village of Mġarr, only a kilometre west of Skorba. A footpath strikes off directly below the Skorba boundary fence, passing one or two undistinguished Punic tombs on the way. By road one must return to the lower end of Żebbieħ and turn right along the side of the valley. The Mġarr temple, *Ta' Ħaġrat*, is down an alley to the left, opposite the school, but the key to the protective wall is held at the police station, also on the left just before entering the square.

Ta' Ħaġrat is again a double temple, consisting of two adjacent trefoils, though both are less regularly planned and of smaller size than the average. The larger is only 15 metres long internally, the smaller 6·50. Zammit, who excavated them in 1925, interpreted them and their distinctive pottery as degenerate, and therefore late. Evans in 1953, with misleading evidence from a new excavation, placed both at the very beginning of the temple period, regarding them as archaic. The author's re-examination in 1960 on the whole supported Evans's view, but was controverted by further results in 1961. These placed the larger temple firmly in the Ġgantija phase, and the smaller in the succeeding Saflieni phase, where its irregularities must be regarded as either archaistic or provincial. The pottery named after the site is certainly early, and must belong to a pre-temple occupation which has yet to be investigated by digging.

The monument is an attractive one, and the view of its façade, with the dome of the modern parish church (1927) beyond, is both popular and evocative (Plate 28). But little comment is required on its details. The roof to the entrance passage is modern restoration, and the repairs to the uprights can be easily made out. The temple started as an open trefoil, but as at Skorba had its central apse walled off at a later stage. The screens of the side apses probably belong to this later alteration too. The closely fitting stone pavement of the central court with its surrounding bench deserves note.

Plate 28. Ta' Ħaġrat Temple and the parish church, Mġarr

The eastern temple is irregularly lobed and of poorer workmanship.

Mġarr village is a modern one, but no less attractive for that. Its church was the result of voluntary labour, backed financially by offerings of local produce, often in kind. Though its name of 'the egg church' is an exaggeration, it has at least a basis in fact.

The road continues westward, past a 19th century country house, the Zammitello Palace. The architectural influence of the Tower of London and the old Eddystone Lighthouse tempts one to describe it as a folly. At the crossroads beyond, the road south leads to the Santi Gap (p. 128), the lane north to Għajn Tuffieħa (p. 141, unsuitable for cars), and the road ahead plunges spectacularly over the cliffs into the *Ġnejna* valley, and thence to the picturesque Ġnejna Bay. Though nothing is known from the valley floor, the cluster of sites around suggests that the valley and bay were known and exploited in early times as they are today.

To the west lies the headland of *Qala il-Pellegrin*, attached to the higher ground only by a very narrow neck of land. A footpath climbs to its eastern tip from the bay, though access is easier along the level from the Santi road by way of Ta' L-Abatija and Fomm ir-Rieħ. Near the highest point of the promontory was a large Roman site, but a rectangular rock-cut cistern is its only notable surviving feature. A loop of cart-rut surrounds the headland, interrupted on the western, seaward, side by cliff falls, which have removed a 100 metre stretch. Near the centre of the southern slope are the tumbled blocks of a temple period building, too ruined for the plan to be recovered despite recent investigation. Another temple period site lay below the cliffs towards the bay. It consisted only of a scatter of sherds on the surface, perhaps from one of the missing settlements, but research here has been inconclusive. Between the cliffs and Ras il-Pellegrin to the north is a tract of startling scenery, where the upper limestone, undermined by erosion of the blue clay, has slid, cracked and jumbled into an extra-ordinary landscape.

The cliffs above Ġnejna Bay to the east are crowned by one of the Knights' watchtowers, the Torri *Lippija*. Another megalithic site lies a short distance to its north. Erosion and flaking of the cliff lip have left nothing but a few scattered blocks, with temple period sherds around,

Plate 29. Għajn Tuffieħa Bay and the promontory of Qarraba

but the position is a magnificent one. Again, a footpath climbs to it from the beach, though the lane above the cliffs is a much easier approach.

Finally the bay is closed to the north by another rocky promontory, *Qarraba* (Plate 29). This small cliff-girt plateau immediately promises a Bronze Age village site, and a few sherds on the almost bare rock of its top confirm this. There is now no easy access—there must have been many rock falls since it was occupied. Paths follow the slopes above Ġnejna and Għajn Tuffieħa Bays to reach the saddle which approaches it, but thereafter one must resort to rock climbing. One route is up the rock face in the middle of the north side, a second follows a fissure within the cliff towards the north-west corner. Both routes are only for the young and active, but the view from the top is worth some effort.

ST PAUL'S BAY AND DISTRICT

The next ridge begins with another fine viewpoint, *Wardija* (Look-out) Hill behind St Paul's Bay. The only remains now to be seen on it are of 20th century anti-aircraft batteries, but occasional prehistoric sherds amongst the modern debris testify to much earlier interest in the site.

There is little further of note until one reaches *San Martin*, where a good road crosses the ridge. It is not the first on the line, as a fine series of cart-ruts score the rock immediately to the east of the road where it crosses the ridge. They descend like the modern road into the head of the small and pleasant valley of San Martin, but are there lost in fields. At this point is a cave, now a shrine of Our Lady of Lourdes. One would like to know to what earlier uses this commodious cave was put. As the road curves out of the valley, one is surprised to find a steam of running water beside it, being carried to irrigate a wide area of fields below. It comes from a prolific spring which breaks out at the junction of limestone and blue clay on the slope of *Qala Hill*.

The hilltop is already marked by its shape as a likely Bronze Age settlement, and the spring makes this a near-certainty. Corroboration is not hard to find. As well as scattered sherds, there are a number of bell-shaped pits cut in the rock which, in view of the spring, are more likely to be for the storage of grain than of water. Further, the neck of land to the west was clearly felt to be too broad for safety, and a wall was built to span it, as at Borġ in-Nadur. Only traces of it survive, and though these include no gateways, we know that there were two of these, one at either end of the wall. The evidence comes from a cart-rut which approaches from the west and forks, a branch heading for each junction of wall and cliff lip.

There are more rut groups at Il-Palma and Ta' Mrejnu, repeating the pattern of the modern roads, but both are rather damaged, by quarrying and olive-planting respectively.

The western end of the Wardija Ridge forks. The northern branch leads to another bluff, *Il-Fawwara*, and this repeats the pattern of Qala Hill—a cart-rut approaching it, Bronze Age sherds and traces of a wall. These are even scantier but sufficient to suggest an attached circular tower at the north end. If there are silo pits too, they are masked by the rather more extensive soil cover. The southern branch runs out to Ta' Lippija (p. 139). The valley between the two has one of the island's most copious springs at its head.

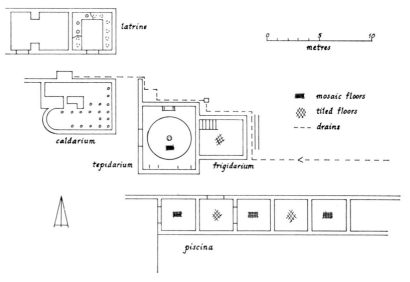

Fig. 26. The Roman Baths at Għajn Tuffieħa

Għajn Tuffieħa, the Spring of the Appletree, has a flow of some 360,000 litres in 24 hours, now mostly channelled into the island's piped water supply. Here the Romans erected an extensive set of baths (Fig. 26). If they are a municipal enterprise of the Roman city of Mdina, it implies that a sufficient water supply for its baths could not be found nearer than this, so that Malta must have been as dry then as it is now. Temple period sherds show that the spring was exploited even earlier, as one might expect, but any structures there may have been then were destroyed by the Roman buildings. These were excavated by Zammit in 1929, and extensive restoration work with UNESCO funds in 1961 has gone far to preserve what survives. The key is kept at the farmhouse down the lane at times when the enclosure is not already open.

The main axis of the site is a tiled passage with water conduit beside it running east–west along the centre of the valley. A row of small rooms south of this, towards the gate, had mosaic and diamond-tiled floors alternately, the remains of the mosaics now protected by low roofs. The westernmost, and best preserved, has a fine pelta and swastika design, and the whole room is completely restored over it. These were probably changing rooms associated with the big *piscina* or bathing pool, only partly exposed, immediately on the right as one enters the gate.

The next three rooms form a series. To the west is the *caldarium*, its floor now missing, supported on tile pillars to allow the heat from a furnace at its north-west corner to circulate beneath it. It has an apsidal west end. Across a passage is the *tepidarium*, fully restored to protect its particularly fine feather-pattern mosaic. This was probably the social centre of the baths, where one could sit in the warmth on the stone benches and converse with other patrons. A stair descended eastwards from this into the *frigidarium* or cold plunge, the necessary prelude to facing the elements after one's bath. North again is a public latrine, unmistakable with its stone seats pierced to a drain below. An unidentified building flanks it on the west.

North of the Wardija Ridge is the *Pwales* valley, easily seen to be the result of faulting. Its eastern end is now flooded by the sea to form St Paul's Bay. As one of the most intensively cultivated areas of Malta, particularly famous for its pumpkins, it is little surprising that it has no ancient sites. The earliest are of the Knights' period, Għajn Rassul (the Apostle's Spring, associated by tradition with St Paul) in the western end of St Paul's Bay village, and the Dellija and Xemxija batteries at the head of the bay. The names of the batteries mean 'shady' and 'sunny' respectively, referring to their positions below the north-facing Wardija slope and the south-facing slope of the *Baida Ridge*.

Ix-Xemxija as a name has spread up the Mellieħa road to include the hilltop above, one of the most interesting corners of the island archaeo-logically. The best approach is by a track along the top of the ridge in the angle of the main road, easy for walking but not recommended for vehicles without caterpillar tracks. The rock here is nearly bare, but the shallow pockets of soil are sufficient to support sheets of the dwarf blue iris, *I. sisirhynchium*, in April, and other flowers in their seasons.

The first antiquity to watch for is the group of cart-ruts which crosses the ridge from Xemxija to Mistra. The ruts of one pair have noticeably rough bottoms and are very shallow, suggesting that they were deliberately pecked to mark them out, but never came into use to be smoothed off by wear.

Higher on the slope (200 metres west-south-west of their plotted position), and much easier to find now that the first has been given an iron grill (key at the National Museum), are the Xemxija tombs. These were excavated by Evans in 1956, to yield a rich collection of prehistoric material (see p. 45). The first interments were made in the Mġarr phase, about 2800 B.C., most fall in the succeeding Ġgantija phase down to 2400, and there is a falling off in quantity towards the end of the temple period, the Tarxien phase. A few pieces testify to later sporadic use down to medieval times.

The tombs vary in complexity. The simple basic plan is shown by Tomb 6 (Fig. 27), for example, consisting of a circular shaft 85 cms. deep, from which opens a kidney-shaped chamber, flat floored and dome-roofed, 3·80 metres across and 1·20 metres high. In this were placed the dead in a crouched position, on one side with the knees

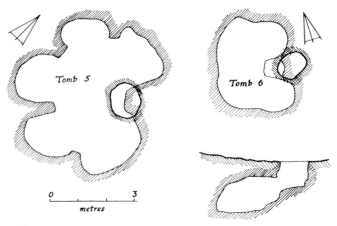

Tomb 5

Tomb 6

0   3

metres

Fig. 27. Xemxija, plans of two of the tombs

drawn up to the chest, together with a few pots and perhaps a polished stone axe-amulet. Tombs 3 and 4 are very similar. By contrast, Tomb 5, under the grill, was made much larger by the cutting of lobed extensions from the main chamber. Its greatest breadth is nearly 6 metres. Any danger of roof collapse was prevented by leaving pilasters between the lobes to support the overlying rock. Tombs 1 and 2, the chambers of which run into each other below ground, have intermediate forms. It is the lobed type which may have been ancestral to the built temples (p. 25).

The settlement where the occupants of these tombs lived before they joined their ancestors has not been found, though there are at least two possibilities. Large sherds of contemporary pottery have come to light in the broken rock below the cliffs to the north, overlooking Mistra. They might represent domestic refuse pitched over from a village above, but erosion has swept this area bare. A cave in a reef of rock south-west of the tombs might also have been inhabited, but it too now has a bare rock floor. An artificial cutting in the rock nearby might have been its water supply.

Another temple period building once stood on the ridge 500 metres west of the tombs, beyond the rocky path which drops back to the Xemxija Battery. A few blocks and sherds, swamped in smilax and prickly pear, are all that survives to show for it.

Westward, interest centres on two hamlets of cave dwellings, some still occupied, and several rut groups, particularly where the two classes of monument are associated. Below the pumping station on the San Martin–Mellieħa road, ruts run out along a rocky shelf which stops at a large cave mouth. This is now empty, not only of modern occupation but of any original deposit. Half way to Manikata, ruts appear to stop at the lip of the cliff immediately above the caves which are still lived in. The loads they carried presumably completed their journey by rope. An elaborate rut group can be traced on the ridge immediately west of the Għajn Tuffieħa–Mellieħa road above Manikata, opposite the new church. The church itself betrays the architectural influence of the prehistoric temples.

Before we leave the St Paul's Bay area, a word would be appropriate on Selmunett, or *St Paul's Islands*. According to the firmly held tradition, this is the site of the shipwreck which brought Paul to Malta on 10th February, A.D. 60. The erection of the apostle's statue on the larger island nearly a century ago, and the climax of the nineteenth centenary celebrations held here in 1960, alike proclaimed it. But 16th century maps are much less specific in their placing of the site on the Maltese north coast, so the tradition would not appear to be very ancient. Indeed in 1952 a Dr Burridge made out a good case for placing the wreck at the head of Mellieħa Bay rather than here. However, unless aqualung divers can bring up a passenger list, or perhaps a lead tag reading 'Paul of Tarsus, Not Wanted on Voyage', we are unlikely ever to attain certainty.

MELLIEĦA

The Mistra valley and *Mellieħa Ridge* have little to detain us. Temple period sites were recorded south-west of Mellieħa and on the foreshore at Għajn Żejtuna to the north, but both have disappeared, through quarrying and wave action respectively. The Selmun Palace is a fine example of a Knight's country residence. On the left side of the lane west of the palace, which descends to a little bay at Mġiebah, is a good example of an old 'bee-house', another fragment of 'industrial' archaeology. It consists of a doorway running into a passage parallel to the façade, which is pierced with rows of holes. Each of these held a pottery beehive on its side, cylindrical with a small hole to the exterior and a large one to the passage. The bees used the smaller; the larger was blocked with a tile until the owner wished to remove the honeycomb.

Mellieħa Bay has, indeed, produced evidence of Roman wrecks, even if St Paul's has not yet been identified among them. Their sites, masked by sand and the growth of *Poseidonia* weed, have yet to be fully exploited. The beach is divided by a rocky point on which another pair of cart-ruts can be traced, submerged by the present sea level at one point (compare p. 84). The longer northern stretch of sand is backed by Il Għadira, the Swamp, which can still in the winter months fill with water and attract migrating waterfowl. It was an earlier and larger version of this lagoon, Burridge suggests, which provided the second of the 'two seas' mentioned in the Acts of the Apostles.

The Marfa Ridge has a number of Knights' defensive works, covering the many bays where hostile landings could be made. There was at least one temple period site, to the right of the main road where it crosses the crest of the subsidiary ridge 500 metres north of the Armier road junction. Large blocks define a round chamber, possibly but not necessarily the last surviving apse of a temple. The road terminates at the main landing place for the Gozo ferry.

6 · GOZO

Gozo, as any Gozitan will insist, is different from Malta. Partly this is a matter of structure, its typical flat-topped hills giving a quite different scenery. Partly it is due to the slower pace of development here, Gozo today being much more like the Malta of half a century ago. Its antiquities, however (Fig. 28), are very similar to those of the larger island, and in two instances at least as good as anything Malta can show. Comino, dividing the channel between the two, has no upstanding remains earlier than the impressive Wignacourt Tower of 1618.

Gozo's harbour is the picturesque bay of Mġarr, at the south-east corner of the island, beneath the walls of Fort Chambray, 1749–61. But any description should begin at the old capital in the centre of the island, 5·5 kilometres to the north-west.

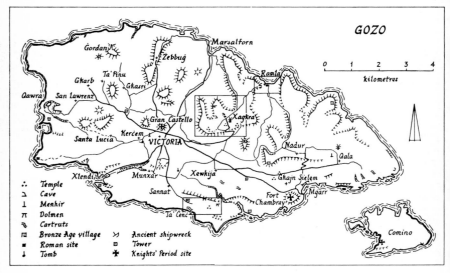

Fig. 28. Gozo, the archaeological sites

Plate 30. The Gran Castello, Gozo, from the east (*above*)—from right to left the Torri ta' San Ġwan, the Cathedral, Casa Bondi and the clock tower, and a view north-east from the walls (*below*), across to the Xagħra plateau

THE GRAN CASTELLO AND VICTORIA

Of the Gozitan hills, that crowned by the Gran Castello is, from its convenient size and strategic position, clearly marked as the capital (Plate 30). Unfortunately this has meant dense and continuous occupation, and the trial excavations so far have revealed nothing on the site earlier than medieval, although we have evidence from It-Tokk (p. 152) suggesting that its origins go back at least to the Bronze Age. It is still the obvious starting point for the visitor, because of the magnificent panorama of the island it offers, for the remains of the Knights' period, and not least for the Gozo Museum, housed in the Casa Bondi within its walls.

The walls themselves are the most noteworthy feature, dating from the 16th to the 18th century (Plate 30). They were intact until the cutting of the new entrance in 1958. Note the Roman inscription on the block built into the old gateway, and the sally ports behind the Casa Bondi. The walk round the walls can be completed in a few minutes, or can be spun out over a couple of hours, by moonlight even longer. The greater part of the island is spread out for inspection beneath—the busy town of Rabat-Victoria, the empty slopes of Il Għelmus with the western hills behind, the farming land in the valley towards Żebbuġ, the misnamed Vulkan (another flat-topped hill reduced to a mere cone) above Marsalforn, the very rich plateau of Xagħra (p. 157), the central plain around Xewkija with, on a clear day, much of Malta beyond, and finally the block of Ta' Ċenċ (p. 161) cutting off the southern sea.

The *cathedral*, designed by the same architect (Lorenzo Gafà) and built around the same date (1700) as that of Mdina, should not be missed. It has an amusing 'dome' painted on its flat ceiling. The old prisons (key at the law courts) and the Torri ta' San Ġwan (St John's Tower), the old keep, are also worthy of note. But the *Casa Bondi*, just inside the old entrance, is essential to any visitor interested in Gozo's antiquities (Plate 31).

The house itself was built by a well-to-do family in the 17th century. Like much of the city it had slipped into ruin, until sensitively restored in 1935 by Sir Harry Luke, the then Lieutenant-Governor. It became Gozo's museum in 1959 (Fig. 29). The hall contains old prints of the island, an attractive if rustic medieval relief of two saints, and a few of

Plate 31. Casa Bondi: the entrance

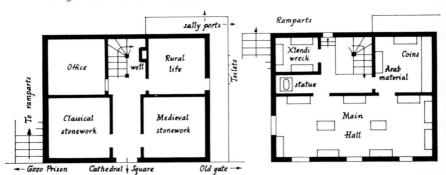

Fig. 29. The Gozo Museum, Casa Bondi

Plate 32. Casa Bondi: the staircase. The amphorae were recovered from the Xlendi wreck

the amphorae from Xlendi (pp. 110 and 163) (Plate 32). The room to the north of the entrance is devoted to Roman remains, fragments of statuary, inscriptions and an olive pipper (compare the restored one in the Roman Villa Museum, p. 109). The room opposite has medieval pieces, notably the inscription from, and careful drawings of, the Gurġon Tower at Xewkija, destroyed to make an emergency landing strip in 1940. The room behind it has a few interesting agricultural implements, a cotton gin (cotton was one of the islands' most important exports for many years), model *luzzo* (fishing boat), etc.

Upstairs, the main collection is in the long room across the front of the house. The centre tables have relief models of the island, with the antiquities marked, and of the 'Inland Sea' at Qawra. The wall cases display material from the major Gozitan sites, Santa Verna, the Ġgantija and Pergla at Xagħra, all of the temple period, Bronze Age from In-Nuffara, Roman from Victoria (Fig. 30), Ramla and Comino. The stone betyl and the snake relief are from the Ġgantija.

By the head of the stairs, a Roman marble statue of high quality is displayed. It is of early imperial date. Whether the slightly larger than

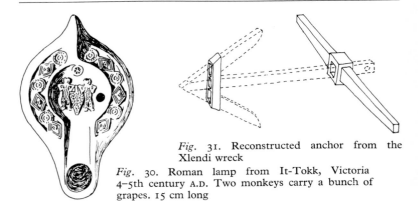

Fig. 31. Reconstructed anchor from the Xlendi wreck

Fig. 30. Roman lamp from It-Tokk, Victoria 4–5th century A.D. Two monkeys carry a bunch of grapes. 15 cm long

life-size figure represents an empress or a goddess is uncertain in its damaged state. The small room beside contains a representative selection of the great quantity of material recovered in 1961 from the sea-bed at the mouth of Xlendi Creek (p. 163). One sherd of Early Bronze Age pottery could have been lost overboard from a fishing boat. A much greater tragedy was the foundering of a merchant ship about the 2nd century B.C. Some threescore whole or fragmentary wine jars, coming from Italian, Greek, Spanish and Punic ports, were recovered from its cargo. Note also the lead anchor stocks (Fig. 31). A few jars are of substantially later date and Byzantine connections, probably from another wreck in about the 5th century A.D.

The remaining room has a selection of coins from the island, including a few from the short period in the 2nd century B.C. when Gozo had its own mint. Most, however, belong to the Roman and Knights' periods. The Arab period is represented by some pottery of North African affinity and the magnificent marble tombstone of Majmuna, a Muslim girl who died in the 12th century at the age of 12 (Plate 33). The stone used had served previously in some Roman building, as the carving on its back shows.

Though the Gran Castello contained the medieval town, it was only the citadel of the Roman one. The town of Rabat, renamed Victoria in the last century, was included within the Roman walls, which crossed Racecourse Street at the main crossroads and followed the lines of Nursery Street and Vajringa Street. There are no visible remains, though traces of masonry of the wall have been noted during rebuilding in

Plate 33. Casa Bondi: Majmuna's tombstone

Nursery Street. However, the antiquity of the city was startlingly revealed in a sewer trench cut across It-Tokk, the main square, in 1960. Natural blue clay was covered by a 3·70 metre depth of artificial accumulation below the modern pavement, a startling contrast to the situation within the citadel.

The lowest level was laid down in the Bronze Age, with sherds of the Borg in-Nadur phase. Then came Punic levels, still fairly thin and without sign of structures in the restricted area available for examination. During the Roman period, however, several buildings had stood on the site. At one point, a cellar still containing wine jars was found, though the jars were empty. A later building had been burnt down, with 5th century A.D. oil lamps left on its floors. As at Mdina, the Arab city apparently shrank within the citadel walls. No later buildings appeared, but the build-up of medieval to recent rubbish, much disturbed by wells, cess-pits, rubbish pits and the like, showed that the town had sprung up again around the square.

The limits of the Roman town are marked indirectly by the discovery from time to time of tombs, which were placed immediately outside the walls. A late Roman catacomb, much damaged, is visible at Kerċem, and another has been recently reported above Għajn il Kbir.

Another relic of the Middle Ages is the group of ledger slabs, gravestones carved with simple symbols but no inscription, supposed to be of the early bishops of Gozo, now built into the wall of St Augustine Square, at the south-west corner of the city.

If the Gran Castello and Victoria, separately or together, have been the island's capital throughout historic times, the distribution map suggests that the centre of settlement earlier was Xagħra. Although it is a pleasant plateau, with good springs below its lip and access to the sea at Ramla and Marsalforn, it is difficult to see why it should have been so markedly preferred to Nadur or Żebbuġ. Heavier destruction of the remains on the other two, or inadequate exploration, cannot be sufficient answer. The prehistoric inhabitants chose Xagħra, and there we must follow them.

The first site is on an outlier of the Xagħra plateau and still falls, rather surprisingly, in the parish of Victoria. Access is by footpath from the Xagħra road as it turns left to climb the slope to the village. *In-Nuffara* is marked immediately by its topography as a likely site for a Bronze Age settlement, and surface remains bear this out. Borġ in-Nadur phase sherds are freely scattered across its surface, and several bell-shaped cisterns or silo pits can be seen cut in its rock. One excavated in 1960 yielded a wealth of pottery and domestic rubbish, dumped there after the pit had gone out of use.

The next fork to the right, clearly signposted, leads to Gozo's most famous site, the Ġgantija.

THE ĠGANTIJA

The *Ġgantija*, or Giants' Tower, is easily the most impressive of the island's temples. It stands on the lip of the Xagħra plateau (100 metres north-west of where the D.O.S. map places it) facing, like so many of the temples, towards the south-east. Its presence has been known for a long time, and even before any excavation was done on it, Jacques Houel in the late 18th century was able to give quite a good plan of it. Clearance of the site (excavation would be a misleading word in the context) was undertaken in 1827, and we are extremely fortunate to have a series of watercolours of the site painted within a year or two of that date by the German artist Brocktorff. The paintings are now in the Royal Malta Library in Valletta, and are practically our only record of the work.

On closer inspection, the pile of masonry can be seen to enclose not one but two temples, both built in the Ġgantija phase (Fig. 32). The

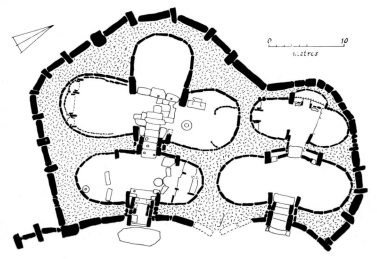

Fig. 32. The Ġgantija Temples

southerly one, on the left, is the older and the better preserved. The façade towards the left-hand corner still stands, unrestored, to a height of 6 metres (Plate 34). Note here the contrast between the rough coralline limestone of the external walls and the softer well-tooled globigerina employed in the walling of the entrance passage and elsewhere inside the monument. The great stone threshold slab deserves mention too.

The plan of this temple incorporates five large apses. The first on the left shows well the composition of its *torba* floor (see p. 135). Traces of the plaster which once covered the irregular walls still cling between the blocks. Fallen fragments in the fill show that it was painted a deep red. There is a good example of one of the holes we suppose to have been used for libations.

The right-hand apse has much more in the way of internal fittings. With the light striking at the right angle, most of the altar blocks can be seen to have carved relief spirals like the better-preserved examples from Tarxien. These were very much clearer in Brocktorff's day, interesting evidence that they must have been protected from the weather by some sort of roof at the time the temple was in use. A fire-reddened circular hearth area can be made out in front of the blocks.

Plate 34. Ġgantija: the façade (*above*) and threshold and central passage of the South Temple (*below*)

Bar-holes can be seen on the inner side of both passages to secure them.

The inner apses are even larger, measuring 23·50 metres from end to end. The central one is floored at a higher level, behind a slab decorated with pitting. This again parallels the first temple at Tarxien. On the paving immediately in front of this block, engraved symbols can be made out in certain lights, camouflaged by lichen growth. They have been read as a Phoenician invocation, but a more sceptical approach is probably safer. Other authorities have suggested that they look very like what someone knowing little or no Phoenician might produce if he wished to add a 'Phoenician' inscription to a site which, until this century, was attributed to that people.

The inner left apse is one of the most startling for its area and height, 85 square metres within 6 metre high walls. The built altar across its back is a little misleading in its present form, but closer inspection will soon show which are the neatly squared modern blocks added to support the ancient cracked slabs. The opposite apse has little of note apart from a second hearth at its centre and traces of an altar niche in the left-hand corner.

Between the entrances of the two temples, the façade has crumbled, revealing in section the original outer wall of the southern temple, later masked by the addition of the northern one. This is of the typologically, and in this case stratigraphically, later 4-apse form, with its central apse reduced to a mere niche. Its overall length internally, from outer end of passage to back of niche, is only 19·50 metres, against the other's 27.

The first and larger pair of apses has a unique feature in the slabs which flank the inner passage. These are neatly tooled to present a slightly concave surface in both horizontal and vertical planes, and are carefully detached from the masonry of the wall behind. The inner apses have altar niches to left and centre, and a raised floor cut from bedrock to the right, mirroring on a smaller scale the arrangement in the adjacent temple. In the wall of the left apse can be seen one block presenting a vertical edge as if thrust through from the back; it is one of the slabs of the first temple's outer wall, allowed to remain when this section of the wall was demolished to make room for the second temple.

The boundary wall is in itself one of the most striking parts of the monument. The great slabs, up to 5·50 metres long, are perched on edge, alternately flat in the wall and with their faces exposed, and projecting radially to give stability to the structure. The term 'long and short work' would describe the technique well, but for the fact that it is already in use for a rather different arrangement of masonry in Anglo-Saxon architecture.

Important though the temples obviously were to their makers, the Ġgantija shows as clearly as Mnajdra did that the religious activities did not stop at their front doors. The concave façades, here somewhat obscured by the tumble, hint at this. The continuation of the façade to the south on the same curve, in the 'long and short' technique, is even more explicit. Conclusive is the great terrace wall on the lip of the slope. If one peers down at its face, typical prehistoric megalithic blocks can be seen to form a substantial part of its lower courses, though later rebuilding in smaller rubble has been necessary too. Excavation in 1953 confirmed that this terrace belongs basically to the temple period, though later than the temples themselves. The effort involved in its construction must imply that this great forecourt played a prominent part in the rites. Indeed the temples may only have been sanctuaries, from which the general public were excluded.

The terrace wall could have had an additional function, as a façade itself. At its foot, rising through the prickly pears, is a single standing stone. Brocktorff shows this as one upright of a free-standing trilithon. An Italian visitor some thirty years earlier wrote a frankly garbled account of some cave beneath the Ġgantija. If this were a hypogeum like that of Ħal Saflieni, and where better in Gozo than underneath its main temple, could this trilithon mark its now walled-up entrance? But stripping of stretches of the modern terrace wall in 1953 revealed only undisturbed temple period deposits. If there is a hypogeum somewhere here, it awaits a future investigator.

XAGHRA

The Ġgantija is only the first and best of a dense scatter of sites across the Xaghra plateau (Fig. 33). A cave was found just to its north in 1949. It yielded an extraordinary quantity of Tarxien phase material, at which time it seems to have served as the temple rubbish tip.

Three hundred metres to the west, just beyond the new road into the village, once stood a second temple. One apse can still be traced. A small cave beneath it, *Ghar ta' Ghejżu*, produced a quantity of Ġgantija phase pottery in 1933.

In the fields west again are traces of what appears to have been a very

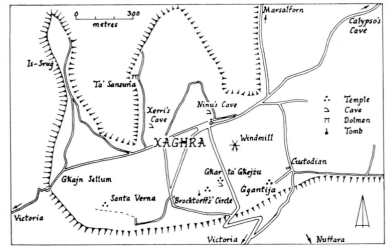

Fig. 33. Xagħra and its sites

important site. Colt Hoare noticed it in 1790. Brocktorff in 1827 painted a large stone circle here, with attached structures, but a few blocks of stone built into field walls and a thin scatter of sherds among the crops are all that one can find today. Here too in 1912 Dr Zammit was hastily summoned by the police when two tomb chambers full of bones and blood were discovered by a farmer. The 'blood' was a sludge of red ochre and water and the bones were 4,000 years old. One tomb is still accessible.

Seven hundred metres still further west is the site of *Santa Verna*, approached by a footpath from the south-west corner of the village. The picture is the sad, familiar one of scattered blocks and sherds, but Peet and Ashby in 1908 excavated enough of the original floor to give, with the standing stones, the plan of a trefoil temple. Three small trenches in 1961 showed that it had been built over earlier occupation levels, going back to the beginnings of human settlement on the islands.

There are three northern spurs to the Xagħra plateau. Three separate scatters of temple period or earlier pottery have been noted on the western one, but nothing survives above ground. On the western lip of the middle one, beyond the entrance to Xerri's Grotto with its stalactites, is the Ġibla ta' Sansuna, probably a partly collapsed dolmen. Another cave with stalactites, Ninu's, lies a few metres north of the parish church. The eastern prong is much broader and longer, ending at the Qortin ta' Ghajn Damma, 2 kilometres from the village centre. This has a Knights' tower and several traces of completely ruined megalithic building. A road from here continues down to Marsalforn.

Eastwards, beyond the Wied ta' Pergla (where another cave with Ġgantija phase pottery was found), is another headland, approached by the lane north-east from the village. In the cliffs at its tip, behind the cottage where the lane ends, is the traditional site of *Calypso's Cave*. One must admit immediately that there is no archaeological support for the identification, and that, if correct, either Homer was indulging in a good deal of poetic licence, or cliff falls have drastically altered the topography since Odysseus's day. The cave is accessible by way of stairs cut in a cleft in the rock, but disappointing. The viewpoint above, however, well repays a visit (Fig. 34).

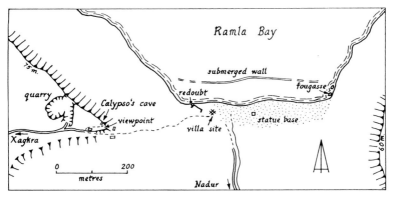

Fig. 34. Ramla Bay, Xaghra and Nadur parishes

Until long-threatened development catches up with it, *Ramla* is Gozo's finest bay, and arguably better than any in Malta either. Its open beach and golden sands (its name means 'sandy') were appreciated from an early date. The mound above the west end of the beach covers the remains of a lavish Roman villa, the country retreat of some wealthy merchant, administrator or landowner. It was dug by Zammit in 1912, and some of the finds, together with a plan, are on show in the Gozo Museum. Wall stumps can still be traced on the ground. Nearby is a notice telling where life-saving equipment for the beach is kept, at Nadur 4·5 kilometres away and 140 metres above sea-level.

But in times of trouble, Ramla could be a threat too. It provides one of the best illustrations of the precautions the Knights took to guard their coasts. Immediately above the villa are the remains of a redoubt, with embrasures for three cannon covering the seaward approaches. A wall was built to span the bay beneath sea-level, visible from above as a dark line when the sea is not too rough. This was intended to hold up boats landing an invading force until the fougasse (see p. 131) in the isolated rock at the east end of the beach could be discharged. However, when the French under Vaubois entered the bay in 1798, the redoubt had a skeleton garrison only. Half of it ran away and the other half surrendered himself without a shot. So ended ingloriously the Knights' rule of Gozo.

EASTERN GOZO

The centre and east of the island have a few sites, but of no great importance. Some sort of temple building immediately east of *Xewkija* church was investigated in 1904, but there are no upstanding remains. There are also cart-ruts along the slope south-east of the village.

Five hundred metres north-west of *Għajn Sielem* village were two megalithic sites, on either side of the Xewkija–Qala road. Neither has a recognizable plan surviving. Li Mrejżbiet, beside the lane into the village, might repay further work, but Borġ il-Għarib to the north is reduced to a few scattered blocks only.

Compared with the wealth of Xagħra, Nadur, topographically so similar, is disappointingly blank. The Torri ta' Kenuna, immediately above the last two sites (used as a semaphore station for communicating with Malta early in the last century), and a Knights' tower on Il Qortin are the only known antiquities.

Qala is only a little better off. A single standing stone behind the school, north-west of the village, is certainly ancient, on the evidence of temple period sherds picked up around it. Whether it is to be regarded as an isolated menhir like that of Kirkop, or the exiguous remains of some megalithic building, as the 'menhir' of Skorba proved to be on excavation, is not known. There are a few more ruts out towards the redoubt on the eastern tip of the island too.

SOUTHERN GOZO

Here there is more of interest. On the southern lip of the higher ground around Victoria is another temple site, *Ta' Marżiena*, 150 metres south-east of its position on the D.O.S. map. A path opposite the windmill tower on the lane between the Munxar and Sannat roads leads to it. No digging has been done here, but the plan of two apses can be made out, from which the layout of a 5-apse temple can be inferred, although much obscured by carob trees.

Ta' Ċenċ beyond Sannat is even more worth a visit (left fork at Sannat church, straight through the arch of the Sannat Palace and past the Knights' tower) (Fig. 35). This rocky plateau, despite its 145 metre

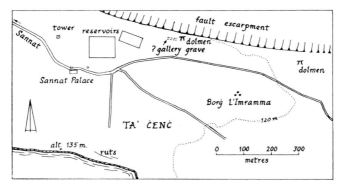

Fig. 35. Ta' Ċenċ, Sannat

altitude, is lower coralline limestone, upfaulted to make the bare escarpment of Sannat and the sheer sea cliffs to the south. The antiquities are concentrated on the eastern end of the plateau. A short distance east of the reservoir and on the lip of the escarpment is a clear dolmen chamber. Just west of it, some standing slabs of stone suggest a megalithic gallery grave, unique in Malta but similar to examples in Sardinia and the heel of Italy. Confirmation would be difficult when so little structure, or soil, survives.

A second dolmen can be found with a little trouble built into a field wall 600 metres further east, and another has been reported 300 metres to the south of that. Much easier to locate, 400 metres south-east of the first and midway between the two lanes, is the temple site of *Borġ li Mramma*. The style of building and sherd scatter confirm a date in the temple period, but the plan is unusual. It consists of a circular court surrounded by small near-circular chambers.

Finally, the bare rock at the top of the sea cliffs shows more cart-ruts. The cliffs themselves are staggering, so the lip should be approached

Plate 35. Xlendi, the Knights' Tower and entrance to the inlet. Diving on the Roman wreck is in progress from the launches to the right

with caution. From one point I have dropped, not thrown, a pebble into the sea 130 metres below. I would recommend anyone repeating the experiment to adopt the same cowardly position that I did.

This block of country is bounded on the north-west by the Wied ix-Xlendi. Plentiful springs at Għajn il-Kbira and below Kerċem make this one of the very few streams in the two islands which flow, after a fashion at least, all the year round. The delightful bay at its outfall, *Xlendi*, has been used as a harbour from very early times, but at least two ships, about the 2nd century B.C. and the 5th A.D., failed to negotiate the reef at its entrance, and sank in 35 metres of water (Plate 35). Their contents, after spending their first night above water level for many years in the security of the Xlendi Police Station's only cell, are now in the Gozo Museum (p. 151). The Knights' Tower stood guard against unwanted visitors to the bay, and the foundations of its 15th century predecessor can be seen above the stream in the angle between the Xlendi and Munxar roads.

Of much earlier date is a rock-cut tomb in the rock between the two branches of the Wied ix-Xlendi above the village. Its opening can be seen near the top of the face towards the road, but access is somewhat tricky.

WEST GOZO

The western third of Gozo was until quite recently known as Il Desert. Population has built up again over the last century, particularly between San Lawrenz and Żebbuġ, but archaeologically the name is still a fair one.

A menhir of unknown antiquity stands on the south side of the Victoria–Kerċem road opposite the Santa Lucia turn. Santa Lucia itself probably took the population of an earlier village on the top of Għar Ilma when that site was abandoned. Unlike Żebbuġ, Xagħra and Nadur, it was too small an area for a viable settlement. Its ruins are clearly traced. Rich Għar Dalam phase material has recently come to light in caves around the plateau of Għajn Abdul, the next hill, but it has yet to be properly investigated.

On the extreme south-west tip of the island, Ras il-Wardija, the Italian Archaeological Mission explored an artificial cave, probably a Roman *nymphaeum* with associated buildings.

Otherwise there is the interesting, indeed exciting, scenery of Cala

11*

Dwejra with the Fungus Rock and the Inland Sea at Qawra. Both are sea-filled dissolution basins like the Maqluba (p. 93). The rock is so called from a fungus with medicinal properties growing only here. It was a monopoly of the Grand Masters, and collected by means of a ropeway, the anchorage for which can still be seen on the tip of the rocky point. The scenery extends impressively below sea level, and the area around, and through, the Portal Rock to the north provides some of the finest snorkel swimming in the islands. Archaeologically the area is a complete blank, though it remains to be seen whether this means that it was avoided in the distant past or merely that the evidence has yet to be found.

The modern pilgrimage church of Ta' Pinu may be left with the last word, testifying as it does to the religious devotion of the Maltese and Gozitans of today, just as the prehistoric temples do to that of the early inhabitants of these islands.

BIBLIOGRAPHY

Many guides to Malta have appeared in recent years, ranging from detailed facts and figures to chatty accounts of visits. I would single out only two, with no disrespect to the rest:

C. Kininmonth: *The Traveller's Guide to Malta*, London 1967 (revised 1970).

Sir Harry Luke: *Malta, An Account and an Appreciation*, London 1949.

Very helpful works on more specialized aspects include the following:

J. Aquilina: *The Structure of Maltese*, Malta 1959 (on the language).

B. Blouet: *The Story of Malta*, London 1967 (on the history).

H. Bowen-Jones, J. C. Dewdney, W. B. Fisher: *Malta, Background for Development*, Durham 1960 (geography, economics, sociology).

Quentin Hughes: *The Building of Malta, 1530–1795*, London 1956 (architecture).

Quentin Hughes: *Fortress, Architecture and Military History in Malta*, London 1969.

H. P. T. Hyde: *The Geology of the Maltese Islands*, Malta 1955.

B. L. Rigby: *The Malta Railway*, Oakwood Press 1970.

E. Schermerhorn: *Malta of the Knights*, London 1929 (history).

More specifically on the archaeology, the best general work at present is:

J. D. Evans: *Malta*, London 1959.

Others of narrower scope or more specialist approach include the following in order of publication:

T. Ashby and others: Excavations 1908–11 in various megalithic buildings in Malta and Gozo, *Papers of the British School at Rome*, VI, London 1913, pp. 1–126.

M. A. Murray and others: *Excavations in Malta*, 3 parts, London 1923–9.

T. Zammit: *Prehistoric Malta, the Tarxien Temples*, Oxford 1930.

J. D. Evans: The Prehistoric Culture Sequence in the Maltese Archipelago, *Proceedings of the Prehistoric Society*, XIX, Cambridge 1953, pp. 41–94.

H. S. Gracie: The Ancient Cart-tracks of Malta, *Antiquity*, XXVIII, Cambridge 1954, pp. 91–8.

J. D. Evans: The Dolmens of Malta and the Origins of the Tarxien Cemetery Culture, *Proceedings of the Prehistoric Society*, XXII, Cambridge 1956, pp. 85–101.

D. H. Trump: The Later Prehistory of Malta, *Proceedings of the Prehistoric Society*, XXVII, Cambridge 1961, pp. 253–62.

Cagiano de Azevedo, S. Moscati and others: *Missione Archeologica a Malta. 1964–*, Rome 1965–.

D. H. Trump: *Skorba and the Prehistory of Malta*, Society of Antiquaries Research Report XXII, London 1966.

J. D. Evans: *The Prehistoric Antiquities of the Maltese Islands*, London 1971.

Local guidebooks of varying value are available for many of the sites. They are inexpensive and often amusing. Where their facts, and even more their interpretations, differ from those in the preceding pages, the author holds to what he has written here. His own *Guide to the Archaeological Section of the National Museum*, for example, is already seriously out of date in places.

INDEX

INDEX